66 FREE Ways To Promote Your Small Business

66 FREE Ways To Promote Your Small Business

The PR handbook for SMEs, entrepreneurs and start-ups

Nick Rennie

Orders: Please contact Nick Rennie.

You can also order via the e-mail address: nrennie157@gmail.com

ISBN: 978-0-9933928-1-8

First published 2016

Copyright © 2016 Nick Rennie. All rights reserved.

All rights reserved. Apart from any permitted use under UK copyright law, no part of this publication may be reproduced or transmitted in any form or by any means, electronic or mechanical, including photocopying, recording, or any information, storage or retrieval system, without permission in writing from the publisher or under licence from the Copyright Licensing Agency Limited. Further details of such licenses (for reprographic reproduction) may be obtained from the Copyright Licensing Agency Ltd, Saffron House, 6-10 Kirby Street, London EC1N 8TS.

Printed in Great Britain for Nick Rennie by 4edge Limited

Contents

Introduction	vii
Chapter 1: Engage with journalists on newspapers & target magazines	1
Chapter 2: Establish yourself as a 'Voice of Authority' within your profession	11
Chapter 3: Leverage the power of Twitter	18
Chapter 4: Build a team of 'brand ambassadors'	36
Chapter 5: Get online savvy	43
Chapter 6: Network with other businesses	55
Chapter 7: Get the most out of Facebook & YouTube	63
Chapter 8: Get involved with your local community	75
Chapter 9: Write regular blogs	82
Chapter 10: LinkedIn, Instagram & Pinterest	89
Chapter 11: Social media best practice	99
Chapter 12: Thinking outside the box	108
Extra Resources: Templates for writing great press releases & business blogs	124

Introduction

I decided to write this book because so many people are now electing to start their own business but many have no idea how to promote it.

Money can be tight with any start-up and some entrepreneurs decide not to set aside a budget for public relations because they consider it a luxury.

This is a huge mistake since the one thing you need to achieve when you launch a new business is to get it noticed by potential customers and clients.

Those who do decide to bring in help from a public relations agency often get disillusioned when they see no great return from what can be a sizeable cash outlay.

In fact, there is absolutely no reason why the owners of small and medium-sized businesses shouldn't take on the responsibility of promoting it themselves.

I am going to show you how easy it is to publicise your new products or services without spending any money at all on advertising or PR.

The only investment required on your part is time. But this is a small price to pay when you see the impact of implementing the ideas I am going to discuss in the following pages.

Getting coverage in newspapers and relevant trade magazines remains hugely important with the added bonus that any articles will not only appear in the printed issue but also online on the publication's website.

I will explain in detail how to write a press release so that it grabs the attention of the journalists you want to impress.

I'm an experienced journalist myself so I know exactly what content will be used and which copy will be instantly rejected.

You can easily get a free editorial feature printed about your business and when you consider the cost of an advert these days it is well worth putting in the effort to make it happen.

Social media also provides countless opportunities for a business owner to get their message out to customers.

Platforms such as Twitter, Facebook and LinkedIn are incredibly powerful in terms of engaging positively with a client base.

And I will outline exactly why in these pages.

I'm aware that many struggle with social media so I will explain the principles of setting up accounts and using them effectively in the simplest possible terms.

There are also plenty of other top tips on how to promote a small business or a start-up. Some will appear simple and you will wonder why you haven't been using them up to now.

Other ideas will hopefully inspire you to put them into practice and begin making a much wider audience aware of what you have to offer.

I've written the book in such a way that readers can cherry-pick ideas as they go along because some will be more appropriate to their business than others.

I have come up with 66 free ways to promote a small business or start-up and every one of them has the potential to make a major difference to your bottom line.

At this point I should explain a little about myself.

I am a public relations consultant who helps raise the profile of clients in a variety of industries and I also work as a freelance journalist in newspapers.

I attained an MA (Masters) degree in Public Relations in 2010 to hone my abilities in that field and I have worked in journalism for more than 20 years.

I am member of the Chartered Institute of Public Relations (CIPR), the professional body for PR practitioners in the UK.

A number of my PR clients have told me they are not confident about sending press releases out to journalists and many also tell me they are left bamboozled by social media.

This was a motivating factor in writing this book because I know how easy it can be to gain press coverage and establish a strong presence online.

Advances in the internet mean it has never been easier to start up a business. This proliferation in start-ups, however, has presented a major challenge for entrepreneurs to get themselves noticed amongst all the competition.

Sometimes it is all about who shouts loudest – in the press or on social media – but I am going to explain that there are plenty of subtle ways you can use to get your message out to customers and clients.

I will assume that readers possess a smartphone – an internet-connected mobile – and they already have a website set up.

And I guarantee you won't have to spend a penny or a cent to implement any of the following ideas.

I hope you enjoy reading the book and I am certain that you will pick up the knowledge to start promoting your business to a much wider audience without spending any money to do it.

Chapter 1

Engage with Journalists on Newspapers & Target Magazines

www.prforsmallbiz.com

1

SEND OUT A PRESS RELEASE TO THE MEDIA

We'll start off with the one every business knows they have to do – the traditional press release to the local newspaper, lifestyle magazine or trade publication.

Now, I know press releases are a source of frustration for many businesses.

When I first speak to clients they will often say that journalists never use the material they send to them. They either don't reply at all or pass it on to the advertising team who then ask for payment.

But there are certain things you can do to give your release the best possible chance of being published as free editorial.

I will go over those points in a moment but first let's look at the structure of your press release. These are the elements you need to have in it:

- A company logo at the top
- A headline to grab the attention of a journalist
- The date the release is being sent out and details of any embargo if you want them to use it only after a certain date
- A strong introductory two or three paragraphs explaining what the release is about and why it is newsworthy
- The main body of the release with some good strong quotes (in normal language and not containing jargon or repetitive mentions of your business name)
- Contact details for yourself with an invitation for the journalist to get in touch with you if they require more information
- 'Editor's Notes' containing information in more detail about the subject matter of the release (this element is optional)
- What is known as a boilerplate at the bottom with basic information about your business, such as when it was founded, where it is based,

which products and services it sells. Keep this brief though – no more than three sentences.

So, you've written your press release and it's time to send it out to the press.

Think about the audience for your release. Is it technical information which would be of more interest to a trade magazine? If it's about a new manager being taken on or an award your business has won then it will also be suitable for the business pages of the local newspaper.

I have tried and trusted protocols which I follow every time I send out a client's press release and I've always managed to get good coverage for them.

Here are my 6 top tips for getting your press release published:

Include an interesting, dynamic subject line in your email
This is crucial because if you don't grab a journalist's attention from the moment your email drops into their inbox then they may never even read it. You are competing with dozens of incoming emails every day so make yours stand out.
Pick the most interesting aspect of your press release and describe it in the subject line as clearly as you can with no jargon.

Target the press release
Send the release to a select number of publications and only those which are likely to be interested in it.
Make sure you email it to a specific journalist. You can find out the name of the business editor of a newspaper or the editor of a trade magazine, for example, via their website or by just flicking through a copy in the local newsagents.

Research each publication you send it to
This is important to get an idea of what kind of articles they publish. For example, a newspaper might have a regular weekly or monthly business section which they will be looking for content for.
In the email you send to each journalist, mention previous recent articles they have carried if they are relevant to your release. A journalist will be flattered that you read their publication and impressed that you've taken an interest, which will improve your chances of getting something in.

Send it well before the deadline
It's vital that you find out when the last copy is accepted by a newspaper or magazine. Don't be afraid to call beforehand to check if you don't know.
In fact, send the release well in advance. If a newspaper publishes on the Thursday each week, then get it to them by the previous Friday so they have plenty of time to use it. Friday will also often be the quietest day for a weekly paper and your article might give them a good start for the following week's issue.
If a newspaper runs business pages every month, find out which week it appears. And be aware that magazines work well in advance, up to two months, so you will need to plan ahead to get content in to them.

Send a follow-up email
Most newspapers and magazines have small workforces nowadays and journalists won't thank you for calling to ask when your press release is going to be used.
Never assume they will use it and never call to ask them if they have received it. Journalists receive dozens of press releases every day and they rarely reply to the sender to say they have received one.
A simple email follow-up a day or two days after you have sent it will suffice. All you need to say is that you sent a press release on a certain date about a particular subject and offer to supply additional information if required.

Call if you don't hear anything after 48 hours
If the journalist hasn't replied to your follow-up email then you are perfectly within your rights to call them.
Once again, don't ask when it is going to appear. Simply explain when you sent it, what it is about and ask if it is something they might be interested in using.
Be aware of deadlines, though. Try to avoid calling when a particular publication is about to go to press.

- If you need extra guidance on writing press releases I have provided some easy-to-follow templates in the 'Extra Resources' section of this book. These can be used across every profession and industry. If you follow the structure I have outlined and also adhere to the six principles above then you should have no trouble in getting good coverage in newspapers and magazines.

2

LOOK FOR POTENTIAL MEDIA STORIES WITHIN YOUR BUSINESS

Publicity for your business in the local newspaper or lifestyle magazine can be incredibly beneficial even if it doesn't involve anything about the products or services you offer.

It's all about raising the profile of your organisation.

It's about planting a seed in the minds of potential customers that you operate in a particular industry and that you might be worthwhile getting in touch with at some point.

So, have a look at your business and the people who are employed in it and look beyond what they do on a normal working day.

You might employ someone who has raised thousands of pounds for charity or who is about to take on a fundraising challenge.

Or another individual could have a very unusual hobby which would make an interesting feature in the media.

Your business might operate from an historic building or one with an interesting backstory.

You are far more likely to spark the interest of a journalist if you offer them something like any of the above than if you are simply telling them about a new product or service, which essentially would be an advert.

The resulting story or feature may only include one fleeting reference to your business or organisation.

But it will help to establish your brand and get its name out there and in the minds of potential customers.

If the piece appears online you will also have the bonus of a boost to your

Google search ranking, since it will be published as unbiased, pure editorial content.

More importantly, telling the stories behind your business, and the people involved in it, will engender real empathy for your enterprise and a certain amount of trust which will more than likely lead to customers and clients investing in your products and services.

3

WRITE A FEATURE ABOUT HOW YOU CAME TO START UP YOUR BUSINESS

An interesting or inspirational backstory will always be of interest to journalists or blog readers.

You often read about entrepreneurs who were virtually destitute before becoming successful in business.

These stories make great copy for the media, as do articles about individuals who spotted a gap in the market and came up with a product or service which makes a real difference to people's lives.

As a business owner you might also be someone who moved to the UK unable to speak much English but you had the drive to become a success in your chosen industry.

The organisation may be family-run and one which dates back generations so tell the media about it and certainly do so if you are approaching a milestone in its history, the 20th, 25th, 30th, 40th or 50th anniversary of the business being founded, for example.

Some individuals have recovered from tragedy to turn their lives around and become successful business people and these stories are also rich in potential for journalists.

The secret is to promote the human side of your business and the people behind it. You will find customers and clients will warm to you far more quickly if they know more about what makes you tick.

If the backstory is particularly interesting you will also benefit from people sharing it widely on social media and really helping to raise your profile across a wider landscape.

4

USE AN ONLINE CLOUD STORAGE SERVICE TO HOST YOUR MEDIA KIT

When you send out information to the press about your business, most journalists prefer it to be sent electronically, via email.

This enables them to cut and paste details straight into their articles and they are able to process images easier if they are in the form of digital jpegs which don't need to be scanned first.

Now, if your news release also contains a big selection of images you run the risk of clogging up a reporter's email inbox if you send them six or seven images at a time.

A great way of getting round this is to use a free cloud storage service, such as Dropbox, Google Drive or OneDrive.

The advantage of this is you can store a selection of high resolution images to do with your business and then create an online link which gives a journalist access to them.

They can then download the ones they want and they are not inconvenienced from receiving huge attachments with your press release.

It is well worthwhile creating a media kit containing generic high resolution photographs showcasing your business together with a press release including all the relevant information about what you do.

Create a folder for your media kit within whatever cloud storage service you are using and this will then be available to send out to journalists easily and efficiently whenever you receive an enquiry from the media.

If you like to send a broad selection of images to the press then you might want to use Google Drive, which offers a whopping 15GB of free storage and is linked to Gmail email.

You get 5GB of free storage with OneDrive, which is linked to Outlook and Hotmail email addresses, and just 2GB with Dropbox.

You can register for free accounts with all of these cloud storage options and then create online links to your media kits or your individual images which can be sent via any email you use for your business.

To access the above apps go to:
www.dropbox.com
www.google.com/drive
www.onedrive.live.com

5

PROMOTE YOURSELF ON THE BACK OF SPECIAL ANNUAL EVENTS

A great way of getting free media exposure is to link your business to a special day or week of the year.

You might be a florist offering something unusual to customers for Valentine's Day or Mothering Sunday.

Or a fitness club instructor who is putting on taster sessions in January at a time when more people commit themselves to getting fit.

Or you may run a pub which is having a special spooky makeover for Halloween night.

Another option is to plan ahead to time a news release around a special national awareness day, such as National Smile Week, National Beer Day, Senior Citizens' Day or Read A Book Day.
The media often runs articles to mark such occasions, particularly if they are quirky days.

And they will want a local link if they are a regional publication or a relevant business link if they are a trade title.

There may well be several of these days which you could link your business to so make a note of them and start thinking about newsworthy ways you can hang a press release on them.

Make sure you find out the copy deadlines for newspapers and magazines so you are able to send them releases in good time for them to be published in the issue closest to the special day or week you are connecting with.

6

WRITE A CASE STUDY FOR THE TRADE PRESS

You will doubtless read a magazine or two which covers the industry you operate in.

A flick through each copy will show that some of the content they publish relates to best practice in a particular profession.

The journalists on these publications are always on the lookout for articles which add value for their readers.

So why not consider supplying some of it yourself? If you have operated in your industry for many years then you are in the perfect position to pass on your tricks of the trade to others.

Case studies are a great way of doing this. Get in contact with satisfied customers and ask them if they would help contribute to a magazine piece which showcases how you have helped them.

Journalists love these human interest pieces which show real life scenarios.

If you are uncertain how to structure a case study then think about including the following elements.

- Introduce your business, what you do and how long you have been doing it for
- Describe a customer you have helped and explain why they approached your business
- Outline how you were able to help them and in what ways it has benefited them as a result
- Repeat this with however many customers you want to include in the piece (I would advise no more than three)
- Ask featured customers if they will consent to you using their name and perhaps including a photograph of them (this adds the important human element to the case study which will appeal strongly to journalists)

Case studies are particular powerful when you operate in a business-to-business (B2B) environment.

Companies you deal with are more likely to read the same trade publications as you so they will be more likely to pick up on any coverage you receive.

Business customers are also probably more amenable to being featured in the press with their name and a photograph since it is great publicity for their brand as well.

Now that we understand how to engage with the media to raise your profile through press stories and features, we will now look at how to build your reputation as a reputable professional in your field.

CHAPTER 2

Establish yourself as a 'Voice of Authority' within your profession

www.prforsmallbiz.com

7

BECOME A 'VOICE OF AUTHORITY' IN YOUR INDUSTRY

There are great advantages to be had from building relationships with journalists so that, eventually, they come to you for quotes on relevant stories.

This can be particularly powerful in trade magazines, which are always on the lookout for trusted sources to comment on topical features.

It is fairly easy to make contact with business editors of local newspapers by networking with them at events and awards ceremonies.

Trade magazines are often based miles away, however, so your best way of engaging with journalists who cover your industry is through social media.

Make a list of all the local newspaper business editors and the reporters who work on the top trade publications and follow them all on Twitter.

Some will follow you straight back but others may require some groundwork. Think about retweeting some of their articles or sending them a tweet where you give some insight into a topic they are writing about.

Slowly, you will make journalists aware of what you do and next time they need a quote for a business feature they could well come to you.

If prospective customers or clients keep seeing your name and business associated with press articles discussing developments in your industry they will begin to regard you as a 'voice of authority'.

The result of this is your start-up or SME will be seen as a beacon of excellence.

A great tip here is to contact the main publications covering your trade and ask for their forward features lists.

Most magazines work a few months ahead and they plan a lot of the content in advance.

You have the opportunity to contribute to these features if you get in early.

8

OFFER TO WRITE A GUEST BLOG ON THE WEBSITE OF A TRADE PUBLICATION

Many magazines are on the lookout for contributions from 'voices of authority' within the industries they cover.

Make a list of publications relevant to your business and have a look at their respective websites.

If they run regular guest blogs make a note of the subjects people are writing about and see if you can offer a piece on an issue which hasn't been covered or which gives a different perspective to a topic which has already featured.

You need to provide added value in your blog and content which will engage with a magazine's readership.

In most cases you will be allowed to include a link to your website and a mention of your company with a brief profile.

So don't worry that you won't be mentioning how great your landscape gardening skills are or how popular your new restaurant or pub menu is because the mere fact that you are appearing as a guest blogger will do wonders for your profile and the public perception of your professional qualities.

Offer to become a regular blogger if there is an opportunity to do so because this will make you and your company continually more visible over a long period and dramatically improve your Google ranking at the same time.

Don't forget to include links to these guest blogs on your social media channels because it will give you valuable extra kudos with your followers.

- Turn to the 'Extra Resources' section at the end of this book for guidance on how to write a great business blog.

9

PRODUCE A SHORT VIDEO PRESENTATION SHOWCASING YOUR BUSINESS

Most of us have smartphones which enable us to shoot high definition videos which can be simply edited and shared with friends and family.

And it is well worthwhile doing this to promote your business too. Potential customers and clients want to see who they are dealing and you can engender a great degree of trust by publishing a professional, engaging video.

Films also work well as dynamic illustrations of what goes on in your business, whether you make goods on a production line, use highly skilled workers or you place a high value on customer service.

You can showcase these important parts of what you do through short videos.

And the key is to make them short. Probably no longer than 90 seconds which is the optimum time you are likely to engage someone to watch online before their attention wavers.

Your videos can be embedded on your website or shared through your various social media platforms.

You Tube is a great free place to promote them, if you have a channel. Presentations where you talk about your business work well here.

See Number 37 in Chapter 7 for how to set up a business You Tube channel if you want to create one.

You can also post short business videos on Twitter. Turn to Number 19 in Chapter 3 for how to go about doing this.

10

CONDUCT A SURVEY AMONG CUSTOMERS ON AN INTERESTING ISSUE IN YOUR INDUSTRY

One of the ways of getting the media interested in your business is to conduct a survey with your customers on a topical issue.

Follow the national and local press to see what stories they are covering related to the industries you operate in.

It doesn't have to be a huge in-depth study. You could send questions to customers and clients on your email database or get them to fill in short questionnaires when they visit.

Once you have a good number of replies and a representative sample, make a note of what the survey tells you and make it the subject of a press release.

Local newspapers will love it, particularly if it reflects the views of people in their catchment area and if it is particularly topical.

If the results are unusual or interesting to a wider audience you can even try sending the release to national newspapers or industry magazines which cover developments in your line of work.

The beauty of conducting a survey which is published by the media is that it helps establish your business as a voice of authority in your field of expertise.

Not only will it raise your profile as a brand but journalists will come back to you for quotes on future stories relevant to the industry you work in.

As with all press coverage you get, make sure you share any online links to the articles via social media to widen the audience for them even further.

11

WRITE AN E-BOOK SHOWCASING YOUR PROFESSIONAL EXPERTISE

Amazon has made it incredibly easy to publish your own book and the best thing about it is it doesn't have to cost a penny.

If you publish an e-book, which can be read on desktop computers, mobile devices or e-readers such as the Kindle, it is a digital document and there are no printing costs involved.

The only investment you will make is the time and effort you put into writing it.

The main benefit of writing a book is the opportunity it gives to establish yourself as a thought leader in your field.

When you try to pitch your services or products to a new client or customer, think how impressed they will be if you can mention the book you have written about the work you do.

For example, an estate agent could publish a book giving tips to property owners on how best to prepare their home, office building or shop unit so that it has the best chance of selling.

A fitness instructor might write about exercise programmes and how to live a healthy lifestyle. Or a music shop owner could write an e-book about what to look for when you are buying a new instrument and how to clean and maintain them.

You don't have to write reams and reams – six chapters should be enough and maybe 5,000 words.

It may sound daunting but you will find that the words will flow if you know your stuff.

Remember to include plenty of contact information for yourself and your business in the book, including telephone number, email and website addresses plus references to your social media accounts.

To publish your e-book on Amazon, follow these steps so you can accelerate your standing as a voice of authority in the field you work in.

- Read the finished manuscript carefully and correct any errors or ask someone you trust to do it for you

- Write a strong title for your book using a phrase which people are searching for online (use the Google Keyword Planner tool – see Number 24 in Chapter 5 to find out how this works)

- Take a good quality image to go on your front cover and add the title and your name – free websites such as www.picmonkey.com or www.pixlr.com will help improve the quality of your cover photo and they are easy to use

- Go to www.kdp.amazon.com and sign up for a free Amazon eBook publishing account

- Follow the simple instructions to upload your front cover and your e-book

- Write an engaging blurb (description of what it is about) for your book and include references to your business and your website address

- It is often a good idea to offer your book for free because you will inevitably get more readers and, as a consequence, make yourself and your business more visible

So you should now be in a position to establish yourself as a voice of authority in your field.
Next we will focus on Twitter, one of the key social media platforms for raising your online profile.

CHAPTER 3

Leverage the power of Twitter

www.prforsmallbiz.com

12

SET UP A TWITTER ACCOUNT TO PROMOTE YOUR BUSINESS

It's essential for small business owners to have a Twitter account and to use it effectively.

You can reach potential clients and customers in real time 24/7 every time you post new content (tweets).

Twitter also allows you to direct valuable online traffic to your website so people can learn more about your products and services.

This social media platform additionally gives you the opportunity to build online relationships with people who might want to do business with you and those who can help promote what you do.

You are limited to just 140 characters but the brevity of posts is why it has become so popular – short, sharp, informative content is what most people look for online.

Getting on Twitter is simple once you go online to www.twitter.com - click 'sign up' at the top on the right and then fill in name, phone number or email address and a password to create the account.

Next is the process of making your profile professional looking and interesting enough to attract followers. The following actions are essential:

- Add a professional looking head and shoulders profile picture of yourself or a logo of your company (never leave this blank because it will dehumanise your brand and make you less approachable and trustworthy online)

- Add an attractive backdrop photo relevant to your business or an interesting view of the town or city where you are based

- Include an online link to your website (it will appear on your profile so customers and clients can easily be directed through to it)

- You have limited space for your bio description so write in plain language what you do and add hashtags (#) to indicate your profession and industry and the town or city where you are based if you rely on a local customer base

Your first two or three tweets should explain all about your business and you should extend an invitation to follow you.

Outline what kind of content you will be posting and state that you are looking forward to sharing it with followers.

You are now ready to start building a following on Twitter and engaging with other users, ultimately to raise the profile of your business.

I have extensive experience of creating Twitter accounts for businesses and organisations and managing them effectively.

These are my top tips:

Post regularly but not too often
There is a balance to be made between keeping your Twitter account active and clogging up the timelines of your followers.
If you tweet too many times and in quick succession people will stop following you.
Think of being stuck with someone at a party who talks too much and becomes very annoying!
I would advise that you tweet at least twice a day, preferably four times and probably no more than six times. That's unless you have a special product launch or you are hosting an event which followers will be interested in. Feel free to keep tweeting throughout those kinds of occasions.
Try to regularly share content about your industry or your professional expertise, whether it is in the form of media articles, blogs or other social media posts.

Limit your promotional tweets
I've worked with some clients who had previously posted only tweets which promote their business. They hadn't engaged with anyone or provided interesting content for their followers.
This is a mistake that new authors often make. They will fire off a succession

of tweets which basically say 'buy my book'.

If you are always promoting your business people will ignore you and eventually unfollow your account. Pushy sales people never succeed on social media.

I am not saying don't post any promotional tweets but limit them to one for every three which are unrelated to your business. Try to remember this one-in-four tweeting rule and you won't go far wrong.

Of course, when you have articles published in newspapers and magazines do go ahead and post online links to them on Twitter. Thank the media organisation which has featured you and include (tag) their Twitter name in the post. It is also worth checking to see if they have tweeted about the article on your business so you can retweet it to your followers.

Make sure you also post links to any blogs you write and content from your website to help drive traffic to it.

Follow relevant Twitter accounts

To help build your following you need to be proactive and follow those individuals and people who can provide a boost for your business.

These might be customers, other businesses you do business with and journalists.

If you rely on a local customer base, it's a great idea to follow as many people and organisations based where you are as you can.

Go to the search bar at the top of your Twitter page and type in the name of the town or city where you are based. A list will come up of local Twitter users for you to check through and follow those you think are particularly relevant. Many of them will follow you back.

By following other local businesses – even those which are not in the same industry – you can share each other's business news. They may even recommend their customers to visit you or your website and you can return the compliment.

Make sure you follow journalists from your local newspaper and lifestyle magazines and also those who write for relevant trade publications. They may well pick up on content you have posted and approach you for press articles or features.

Engage with other users

This is the process of building relationships with people on Twitter. It's called a social media platform for a reason and it relies on users conversing online. By nurturing connections with others on Twitter they are also much more likely to share your content with their followers and endorse what you do as a business.

This third-party endorsement is like gold dust, of course, so do what you can to achieve it.

Engaging at its most basic level involves retweeting something you enjoyed reading on Twitter, although do make sure the content does not reflect badly on your professional reputation.

You should also try to reply to tweets and engage people in conversation. For example, another business might post about an award they have won. Try tweeting back with your congratulations and asking how they got the award.

Someone from your locality might have completed an impressive fundraising feat so you may want to share that and praise what they have done.

Another tip is to ask questions of your followers about local issues or topics which people are talking about in your industry. You may well get a good number of responses and this will help raise your profile locally.

Listen and respond to others
It's a good idea to monitor what people are saying online about your business. Do a Twitter search regularly on your company name. If you come across any criticism of your business don't ignore it because the person who tweeted it will likely have sullied your reputation in the eyes of their followers. Make contact with the individual by replying to their tweet and take the conversation offline by including an email or telephone number for them to get in touch with you. Hopefully, you can resolve the issue and they will post again but, this time, in praise of your company.

You may also get Twitter notifications from others who are unhappy with your product or services or Direct Messages (private posts which can only be seen by you) and in both these cases make sure you respond in the way I outlined above.

Of course, you are hopefully also going to see tweets from users who are satisfied customers or clients. Retweet these and also send a tweet to them thanking them for their kind words and perhaps direct them to another facet of your business which they might be interested in.

13

RESEARCH HASHTAGS FOR YOUR TWITTER POSTS

A Twitter hashtag, for the uninitiated, is a word or a phrase with no spaces following the # symbol. Something like #Fridayfeeling , #smallbusiness or #networking.

When you post a tweet, the hashtags you use will determine how many people actually see it.

If you don't use a hashtag at all then your followers will all be able to see what you've written.

But in order to make your tweet visible to a much bigger audience you need to add at least one, and preferably two, hashtags.

A good tip, before you post anything, is to find out which hashtags are being used around the subject you are planning to comment on.

Go to the search box at the top of your Twitter page and type in a few hashtag keywords relevant to the tweet you are about to post.

So, if you are a pub manager seeking to advertise something you might try #pubfood or #barstaff and if you are a gym manager you could type in #fitnesstips or #warmupexercises.

Then click on each of these hashtags to see how many people are using them and if they have used them recently.

If one of them is particularly popular then you can be sure that plenty of people on Twitter are searching for these keywords and phrases.

There are also websites which tell you the top trending hashtags for particular content – www.hashtagify.me is one of the best of these.

You should also keep an eye on trending topics – the most discussed issues on Twitter at a particular time - which are listed on the left-hand side of your page.

And if you are able to link your business to one of these trending topics then do so.

Twitter users are constantly monitoring trending topics and then following Tweets around those subjects so if you can get your business in there somehow then many more people will potentially become aware of you.

But steer clear of nonsense hashtags. Phrases like #Icantwaitfortheweekend or #thecustomerisalwaysright mean nothing and you can be sure that no-one is searching for them so they add no value to your Tweets.

14

USE TWITTER LISTS TO BUILD A POTENTIAL CUSTOMER BASE

When you open a Twitter account you have the option to divide your followers into lists.

This means you can list customers, other local businesses, suppliers, relevant journalists and even rival companies.

Having a customer list on Twitter effectively gives you a new database to run alongside your customer email database.

The beauty of the Twitter list is you can engage on a regular basis with people who buy your products or your services and build a relationship with them which could well lead to repeat business.

This isn't possible with email which, by its very nature, can only be used sparingly and, almost exclusively, to sell to customers.

By clicking on a specific list you can also see a timeline of tweets specifically from that group of people.

It is really useful feedback for your business because you can pick up on trends and attitudes relating to your industry from the content which is being posted by customers, for example.

By listing rival businesses on Twitter you can also look at how they are using this social media platform and learn from those who are using it well.

You can opt to keep your lists private if you want to. I would advise you do this with your customer list so the customer is not aware you are monitoring them so closely and rival businesses cannot copy what you are doing.

Follow these steps to set up your Twitter lists:

- Click on the 'profile & settings' tab on the top right of your page
- Just below 'Create A List' on the right, click 'create new list'
- A box will come up for you to enter your 'list name' & a 'description' of it
- Choose whether you want the list to be 'public' (available for anyone to see online) or 'private' (only you will be able to see the list)
- You will then see a box for you to search for Twitter accounts to add to your list
- Click follow on the ones you want to add unless you already do follow them
- To add to the list click on the symbol to the left of the 'follow' box (shaped like a sun with rays coming out), then hit 'add or remove from lists' from the drop down menu & finally tick the box of the list you want to add it to from the next drop down menu
- If you already follow a lot of Twitter accounts you can also go to the list of accounts you are 'following' (top left of your page) and you can then go through each account you are following and add them to your list following the same procedure I outlined in the last bullet point
- Finally, go to 'lists' again at the top right from the 'profile & settings', click on the list and you will be able to see either all the accounts in that list (under 'list members' on the left) or a timeline of their tweets (under 'tweets')

15

FOLLOW RELEVANT JOURNALISTS ON TWITTER AND ENGAGE WITH THEM

You can always aim to get editorial coverage in local newspapers or in relevant magazines rather than spending valuable money on advertising.

One of the best ways to achieve this is to build a rapport with journalists who work in publications you want your business to be featured in.

Most reporters and editors are on Twitter because it provides a rolling timeline of news which they can then follow up on to write stories and features for their print and online outlets.

If you are a local business, get hold of copies of newspapers which cover your patch and you will find that the Twitter names of all the journalists are printed in them, usually under a by-line or on a page detailing contact details. You can also source their usernames on Twitter by searching under the name of the publication.

Follow them on Twitter and it is very likely they will follow you back since you could be a source of local news.

If the publication has a business editor it goes without saying that you need to be following them.

It might be harder to find the Twitter names of journalists working on magazines but you could try typing the name of the title in the search box at the top of the page and you will get a list of Tweets, some of which will be from journalists on the publication you are after.

If they follow you back, and most of them will if your business is relevant to them, send them a tweet to thank them for following you.

Engage with them after that initial connection by sending a reply when they have posted a link to a story which is important in your community.

If you have an event or a launch coming up which you think is newsworthy, send them a tweet by including their Twitter name (tagging them) to let them know about it.

Remember, you don't need to keep pushing what you are offering as a business. Simple everyday posts and regular interaction with a journalist on Twitter will do wonders for your profile, both online and in the community.

Once you've established this relationship it will smooth the way for any press releases you send to that newspaper or magazine.

It is no guarantee the journalist will use the release but because you have this connection with them they may well come back to you and suggest how it could be more newsworthy or ask whether you have any other interesting snippets of news for them.

16

ENGAGE WITH A CELEBRITY ON TWITTER OR A PROMINENT INDIVIDUAL/ORGANISATION

Now, we all know about the value of celebrity endorsement. When a popular high profile figure praises a business there are likely to be huge benefits in terms of people looking them up online and buying their products and services.

One of the biggest examples of this I have come across in recent years concerns Nice Pie, a small family enterprise in Leicestershire which makes speciality pies.

They were visited by celebrity chef Jamie Oliver for one of his television shows and after the programme appeared interest in the business went through the roof to the extent where it has now expanded significantly.

Of course, it's not always easy to get a celebrity or a high profile figure to endorse what you do.

But you can use social media to establish highly beneficial links with them. There are opportunities to have posts shared by those in the public eye.

I can give you an example of my own. I was watching the ITV breakfast television show, *Good Morning Britain*, one day and noticed the apparent strained relationship between the hosts Piers Morgan and Susanna Reid.

I tweeted about it probably being good for ratings, knowing it would appeal to Piers and his enjoyment of a reputation as the journalist many love to hate.

And he retweeted it to his five million followers. As a consequence my phone kept beeping with notifications about people engaging with the retweet for the next hour or so.

The upshot was that my original tweet was seen by more than 200,000 people, 2,500 were motivated to engage with it in some way to share it with their followers and 371 people clicked on my profile.

This is a recording of those statistics with my tweet:

Impressions	201,113
Total engagements	2,598
Detail expands	2,068
Profile clicks	371
Hashtag clicks	104
Follows	30
Likes	17
Replies	5
Retweets	3

To make my tweet visible to the presenters in the first place, I included their Twitter usernames so they would get a notification of the post.

To put this into context, an everyday tweet where you have used good hashtags and username handles would result in between 500 and 1,000 impressions (total number of Twitter users who see it) and a handful of clicks on an individual's profile.

Another tweet of mine about a popular Sky TV comedy show called *Rovers* was retweeted by one of the stars, which ensured it was seen by an impressive 34,000 people on Twitter. The analytics are recorded below with the tweet I posted:

Tweet Activity

Nick Rennie @renster157
Loving the new #Rovers on @sky1 -a cross between #EarlyDoors & #TheRoyleFamily with some authentic non-league football characters thrown in!

Impressions	34,463
Total engagements	151
Detail expands	79
Profile clicks	30
Hashtag clicks	29
Likes	11
Retweets	2

Reach a bigger audience
Get more engagements by promoting this Tweet!

Get started

You will see that 151 engaged with the post and 30 clicked on my profile.

These figures are important if you are posting the tweet as a business because it means that 151 people are sharing information about your company with their followers and that 30 are looking at your profile to find out more about you. These may well become customers and clients because they are now aware of what you do.

Below is the Twitter activity from a post I made during the *Rio 2016 Olympics*.

I included the username of the youngest Great Britain medallist and she retweeted it.

Once again you will see thousands of impressions of the tweet, 180 engagements and 16 profile clicks.

Tweet Activity

Nick Rennie @renster157
Youngest #TeamGB medallist @amytinkler2 is 16 & oldest #nickskelton is 58. And both cried on the podium at #Rio2016 !

Impressions	13,191
Total engagements	180
Likes	60
Detail expands	53
Hashtag clicks	38
Profile clicks	16
Retweets	12
Replies	1

Reach a bigger audience
Get more engagements by promoting this Tweet!

Get started

One of the best ways of influencing a high profile person or organisation to engage with your tweet is to include a relevant image.

If you are at a trade show and you come across a celebrity, or you see one at a shop opening or book signing, then take a photograph and post it on Twitter or Instagram. A 'selfie' of you both would also work well, if you get to meet them.

Make sure you include the high profile person's Twitter username (presuming they have an account) and add a few words of praise or just record the fact that you have come across them at the event.

It is very possible they will retweet your post and that others will engage with the photograph. As I have outlined in this book elsewhere, images and videos tend to spark much greater engagement on social media than other types of content.

There is an example below of a photo I tweeted about my niece being a football club mascot:

Impressions	7,842
Total engagements	719
Media engagements	525
Detail expands	81
Profile clicks	58
Link clicks	32
Likes	15
Retweets	6
Follows	2

The post had nearly 8,000 impressions and a whopping 719 people engaged with it, by sharing it with their followers. You will also notice that 58 also clicked on my profile which is a vital part of leveraging the power of social media for a small business.

17

BUILD ONLINE RELATIONSHIPS WITH LOCAL AND INDUSTRY JOURNALISTS

It's not difficult to nurture connections with press reporters, thanks to social media.

In the past, the only contact you would have with a business correspondent or a journalist on a trade magazine was when you were pitching press releases to them or meeting up briefly at awards evenings.

That's no longer the case, though, because you now have the opportunity to build relationships by exchanging posts and comments on Twitter and Facebook.

The beauty of doing this is that the reporters who are relevant to you and your business will be far more likely to use your news items if they already know what you do.

It's a way of smoothing the passage of press releases and it may also encourage them to approach you for quotes if they are writing an article relevant to the industry you operate in.

But how do you build relationships with journalists on social media?

Here are a few pointers which will help you do it:
- Look for the Twitter usernames of journalists on your local and regional newspapers and on relevant trade magazines and follow them (most titles now print them under story by-lines in the print versions or on their website)

- Type in 'business correspondent' in the search box at the top of your Twitter page and follow all that are listed

- If they follow you back, be sure to send them a message back to thank them

- Send a Direct Message (private posts on Twitter) offering your help with any stories they are writing relevant to your industry

- Create a Twitter list for journalists (see Number 14 in this chapter for advice on how to do this) to find out the issues and subjects they are writing about

- Look out for posts by relevant journalists and comment occasionally on them, whether they are business-related or of a personal nature

- Read their articles and retweet and 'like' some of them when links are posted on Twitter

By doing all of the above you will succeed in raising your profile and making your business more visible to journalists who are important to you.

And when you have an important new product launch, an exciting new service to offer or something else newsworthy about your business, there is far more chance that a press release will be used because the relevant reporters already know about you and your professional standing.

18

SEARCH TWITTER FOR POSTS ABOUT YOUR INDUSTRY TO SHARE ON SOCIAL MEDIA

A common theme through this book is the need for you as a business person to establish yourself as a voice of authority in your field, as we touched upon in detail in Chapter 1.

This is not difficult to achieve and by doing so it legitimises what you do and validates the products and services you sell.

Let us take Twitter as an example. If you are a hairdresser you should be looking to follow the accounts of journalists and publications which cover your industry.

Monitor what they are posting and either retweet or share a link to articles which you think your followers (many of whom are probably customers or fellow hairdressing professionals) might be interested in.

This might be content relating to trendy new hairstyles, techniques of hairstyling or new products on the market.

By typing in relevant words in the 'search' box at the top of your Twitter page you will come across posts and accounts from people interested in the industry.

If you are regularly posting content which is informative and which others are also sharing it will do wonders for your reputation as a hairdresser.

As a customer reading your Twitter posts I would instantly think you know what you're talking about. And this perceived professional competence should translate into people wanting to use your services.

Make sure you repeat this exercise across all of your social media channels.

Search and follow journalists and trade publications on Facebook and Instagram, and every other platform you post on, to keep up-to-date with industry trends and developments so you can share them with your following.

Because you are limited to 140 characters on your tweets you need to shorten the links you are sharing to online magazine and newspaper articles.

If you don't, the URL address will eat up most of your allocated characters.

A great way of doing this is to use free online tools such as the *Google URL Shortener* at www.goo.gl or *Tiny URL* at www.tinyurl.com.

Simply enter the web address for the content you want to share and click the box indicated on the right to get your shortened URL address.

Then just cut and paste it into your post.

It will reduce an online address which could have dozens of characters to one of only around 20, leaving you plenty of extra words to use in your business tweets.

19

SHOOT A TWITTER VIDEO TO PROMOTE A REAL TIME EVENT

PR and marketing people place a lot of importance on the concept of 'storytelling' when it comes to promoting a business or brand in today's multi-channel digital world.

This, in essence, means showing the human side of what you do by highlighting the people behind your business, your professional skills and how your work benefits customers and clients.

Social media can do this for us if we use the various platforms effectively.

Twitter recently introduced an option to post video and this is a great tool for storytelling.

It allows you to shoot a short video on your mobile phone where you are talking to the camera or showing something interesting happening.

And you can then post that footage to your Twitter feed in seconds so people see it in real time.

Here are some of the ways businesses can use Twitter video:

- Footage from an open day
- Details about special offers
- Late appointment vacancies
- Demonstrations of how new products work
- An outline of a new service you are providing
- Showcasing your professional skills
- Interviewing a satisfied customer or client
- A tour of a new shop or business premises
- Interview with a new member of staff
- Showing off an award and explaining how you won it

And here is how specific businesses might use Twitter video:

- A beauty therapist demonstrates a treatment on a client
- A coffee shop owner goes through the process of making 'the perfect

Cappuccino'

- An estate agent films a tour of a new property up for sale
- A printing firm's new manager talks about his new job
- A car salesman makes a film showing the inside and outside of a second hand car
- A cleaning firm demonstrates how to get rid of a particular stain
- A shopkeeper talks about a closing down sale
- A hairdresser announces she has a vacant appointment available
- A restaurant's chef makes one of his signature dishes

You can shoot Twitter videos on both iPhone and Android smartphones. They can then be uploaded straight away to Twitter or there is an option to edit them before posting.

To post a Twitter video, go to your Twitter account on your mobile and start a new message.

Tap the camera symbol and you will see the option to shoot video, which is done by tapping and holding down the video camera symbol. Films of up to 30 seconds can be posted to Twitter.

We've looked at how Twitter can benefit your business in a number of different ways.
In the next chapter we will focus on how you can build a team of brand ambassadors to help promote what you do.

CHAPTER 4

Build a team of 'brand ambassadors'

www.prforsmallbiz.com

20

CREATE BRAND AMBASSADORS

Brand ambassadors are basically people who will talk positively about your business to their relatives, friends and work colleagues.

At the most basic level this might be your partner, your children, parents or other family members.

Their endorsement does not carry the same weight, however, as that received from customers and people unrelated to you.

Relatives and friends have a vested interest in you and want to see your business do well, of course.

But people who you only interact with as customers, and who praise your products or services, are extremely valuable ambassadors.

There is no reason for them to falsify their backing for your business. So when they shout about you on Twitter and Facebook it carries an awful lot of weight within their social media circles.

The ultimate result from this is that their friends might check you out online or they could even visit your premises in person to find out more.

Subsequently, they may become customers or clients or, at the very least, they are aware of what you do and may well recommend you to their relatives, friends or work colleagues.

So how do you go about building a team of 'brand ambassadors'? Here are some pointers on how to go about it:

- Ask satisfied customers to follow your business on social media and share some of the content you post with their followers
- Ask satisfied customers to post a review of your business on one of their social channels with a link to your website

- Lobby customers to review your products or services on an online rating site such as TripAdvisor

- Ask regular customers if they would be willing to write a testimonial for your website via an email, perhaps

- In most cases, customers and clients will be happy to help you in this way.

Of course, if your customer service is good then these ambassadors will promote your brand in unseen ways, such as when they are having a meal out with friends, chatting to others parents at the school gates or having a coffee with work colleagues.

Even if you secure just five to 10 brand ambassadors each month it will make a significant impact on your customer base.

21

ASK CUSTOMERS TO REVIEW YOUR BUSINESS ONLINE

People will, more often than not, look for online reviews for a product or service before making a purchase.

And if they find two or three positive comments they are much more likely to become customers.

If you look at books on sale on Amazon, for example, check out how many good reviews the best sellers have amassed.

That third-party endorsement influences others to buy the book and doubtless to leave a review after they've finished reading it.

Of course, reviews can work both ways.

The reputation of a hospitality business, such as a pub, restaurant or hotel, for example, can be heavily affected by a review, depending on whether it was complimentary or critical.

If you are concerned about the impact a review might have, it is probably in your interests to ask only satisfied customers if they would mind leaving a review on a website such as Trip Advisor.

You could do this by giving them a card with their bill and asking them to leave a review on a specific website.

Any positive endorsements you receive in this way can then be used in promotional material. You don't have to refer to the person who left it if you are worried about respecting their confidentiality.

Keep an eye on relevant review websites. Some give businesses a right to reply so you might want to leave a comment of your own if a negative review has been left, to apologise to an irate customer and give a mitigating explanation if there is one. If the bad review was unwarranted you can also put your side of the issue to protect your reputation.

22

SHARE GOOD NEWS OR PROMOTIONAL NEWS OF FELLOW BUSINESS PEOPLE IN YOUR AREA

In any town or city, and a good number of villages, there is a collection of small independent businesses operating.

Some, of course, will be competing for the same customers but many won't be.

The thing they all have in common is that they have a limited budget to promote their products and services.

But a good way round this is to work together. Think about it this way: People who dine at a restaurant or drink at a bar in a particular town will also visit the hairdresser, the dentist and the garden centre. These individuals are also likely to market their property at the high street estate agents, enrol their children at the academy school and buy paperbacks from the book shop. All of these businesses can act as brand ambassadors for each other. They can do this by sharing their news on social media and helping to spread the word online about new premises, new products and new services being offered by someone locally.

This is my seven-step plan for individual businesses to set this into motion:

- Do a Google search for the websites of every local business you can find in the locality

- Find the social media links for those businesses on their sites and follow them on Twitter and Instagram, 'like' their Facebook pages and connect with them on LinkedIn

- Then send a message to them highlighting an area of their business which you find interesting and ask them to link up with you on your social media channels

- Reply to them if they respond, and the majority will do

- Monitor their social posts and retweet the occasional tweet and 'like' their Facebook and Instagram posts now and then

- The chances are they will return the favour so make sure you thank them each time

- Continue to monitor the posts of other local businesses and congratulate them on any good news they have while wishing them well at special times of the year such as Christmas and New Year

The beauty of this, if just a dozen or so small businesses do the same thing, is that they will all be acting as brand ambassadors for each other and promoting what each other does in front of a much wider audience online.

Eventually, business people will be referring their customers to the other organisations which they have nurtured this social media relationship with.

This model of engaging with other small businesses also works on industrial estates, shopping malls and business parks where there are multiple neighbouring enterprises working away in a range of different industries.

23

ENCOURAGE EMPLOYEES TO POST ON SOCIAL MEDIA

One of the best free ways of promoting your business is to encourage staff to post about their working day on the company Twitter, Facebook and Instagram accounts.

This is a great way of humanising what you do and engaging with existing and prospective customers.

You might want to limit the number of people who post and nominate those who are confident about using social media.

And I always advise businesses to put in place a social media policy where multiple employees are posting.

This ensures everyone protects the reputation of the company they work for and that content is posted in the right tone.

This last point is important because the nature of your business should dictate the tone you use for posts on social media.

For example, a hospitality business or a service sector company might mix in the odd light-hearted, humorous comment on Twitter or Facebook.

But an undertaker or a solicitor should adopt a more respectful, professional tone.

Of course, inappropriate content should be avoided whatever your business is.

And it should be emphasised to staff that they must avoid getting into online social media arguments with customers or clients.

Staff should be encouraged to post about personal issues and passions if they are appropriate and likely to be of interest to customers.

Getting across the human side of your business and showing employees as normal rounded people is much more likely to make others want to give their custom to you.

A company social media policy should include the following considerations:

- Nothing should be posted which is likely to damage the reputation of the business

- Posts should be truthful and honest

- Replies to customer complaints should be respectful and professional

- No online arguments should be conducted with customers (send them an email or telephone contact number so the conversation can be continued offline)

- No swear words should ever be used in posts

- Do not share content from other sources where it is likely to portray your business in a bad light

- Never post anything which is derogatory towards competitors

- Staff should observe the same principles above when posting work-related content on their own social media accounts

- All employees who post on social media on behalf of your business should receive a copy of your policy so they are aware of the protocols.

Now that we understand how to build an army of brand ambassadors we will take a look at how you can use the internet effectively to reach potential customers and clients.

CHAPTER 5

Get online savvy

www.prforsmallbiz.com

24

USE THE GOOGLE KEYWORD PLANNER TO GET NOTICED ONLINE

If you want to get noticed on the internet there is a great free tool which tells you exactly which words and phrases people are searching for.

It's called the *Google Keyword Planner*.

Basically, it allows you to fill your website and blogs with content which potential customers and clients are looking for online.

By testing out key words and phrases using this tool, you will be able to find out how many times a month, on average, they are being searched for on the internet.

If you notice that thousands of people are searching for particular relevant things online then you should ensure you include that content in your website copy and your blogs.

By using the planner effectively you can direct plenty of traffic to your company website with the possibility that some of those who visit will become customers and clients.

To get access to the *Google Keyword Planner* go through the following steps:

- Log on at www.adwords.google.com

- Set up your Google Adwords account as prompted (you don't have to buy any advertising but you need an account in order to use the planner)

- Log in to your account and click on 'Tools & Analysis' & choose 'Keyword Planner' from the drop down menu

- You will then be asked which search you want to do so click on 'Search for New Keyword' and 'Ad Group Ideas'

- Then enter words or phrases you want to use on your website or in your blogs

- After clicking 'Get Ideas' you will be shown how many people are searching for that word or phrase online

- There will also be an indication of whether there is 'high' or 'low' competition for the word or phrases

- Ideally you are looking for at least 2-3,000 searches per month for a particular word or phrase and 'low' competition (that is, 2-3,000 people are searching for a word or phrase but not many people are using them on their websites or blogs)

Case study 1
Let's assume you are a *physiotherapist* and you want to promote your treatment of sports injuries.

These are average monthly searches for relevant terms on the *Google Keyword Planner*:

'Knee pain'	201,000
'Knee injuries'	33,100
'Sports injuries'	14,800
'Sports injury clinic'	6,600
'Sports injury treatment'	480
'Sports injury specialist	260

Clearly, you need to include the phrases 'knee pain', 'knee injuries' and 'sports injuries' so potential clients will find you online. In contrast, it's not worth using 'sports injury specialist' as not many people are searching for that on the internet.

Remember to look to see which words and phrases are shown as having 'low' competition as using these will project your content higher up the Google rankings.

Case study 2
Next, let's consider the results of the planner tool from the perspective of a *restaurant owner*.

'Places to eat'	90,500
'Eating out'	60,500
'Seafood restaurants'	135,000
'Restaurant menu'	22,200
'Where to eat out'	90
'healthy dining'	260

It's obvious here that if you specialise in fish dishes then make sure the phrase 'seafood restaurants' is mentioned on your website and your blogs. 'Places to eat' and 'eating out' will also work well in terms of reaching potential customers. And the planner tells us not to bother with the likes of 'where to eat out' and 'healthy dining' in your copy.

Case study 3
Finally, we will look at the *Google Keyword Planner* from the point of view of an *estate agent*:

'Houses for sale'	1,220,000
'Homes for sale'	450,000
'Property'	246,000
'Local estate agents'	1,900
'houses to let'	6,600

The tool tells us that we have to include the phrases 'house for sale' and 'homes for sale' on our website. 'Houses to let' and 'property' should also feature. But there is a surprisingly small number of average monthly searches for 'local estate agents' so that is one phrase you can avoid using.

Whatever the nature of your business, using the Google planner will help you optimise your web copy to make your products and services more visible to potential customers.

The fictional businesses in these case studies would all rely on a local customer base so it would be advisable for them to use the name of the town or city where they are based alongside the keyword phrases highlighted here.

25

LET YOUR OLD SCHOOLS KNOW ABOUT YOUR BUSINESS

This is a much-overlooked way of raising the profile of your business or organisation.

The websites of educational establishments are highly valued by internet search companies such as Google or Bing.

So, any content featured on them will rank high when it comes to online searches.

It follows, therefore, that you will get a massive boost from being featured on the website of your old school, college or university as one of its successful alumni.

It's not advisable just to call the school or college up, however. Offer them something in return. Ask if they would like you to give a careers talk to pupils, for instance, or offer free equipment or services beneficial to the school.

Write a short biography of what your business is about and include some key words and phrases which are search engine friendly for your industry.

Include some memories from your school days and make sure you praise the school as a key influence in making you a success.

Have a look at their website beforehand and see if they have any sections on alumni and, if they don't, perhaps suggest they might like to start one.

Alternatively, the school may have another web page where your business profile could sit, such as 'latest news'.

Find out the name of the head teacher or principal and the person who co-ordinates careers events for them and make sure you send your submission directly to both of them.

26

USE A FREE ONLINE MAILING SYSTEM TO REACH CUSTOMERS/CLIENTS

One of the ways you can keep in touch with existing and prospective customers is online mailing systems.

In basic terms, you can send regular promotional emails, in the form of short newsletters, in bulk to a database of email addresses.

The main advantage is that you can post out these mails to hundreds or thousands of individuals with one click of the mouse.

Those who receive your emails will not see everyone else you have mailed to so it will feel like you have addressed them personally.

People can easily subscribe or unsubscribe to your list if they don't feel the content is relevant to them.

There are a number of platforms which offer this service but the one I have used regularly is *MailChimp*, which is free for businesses providing you have 2,000 or fewer subscribers and you don't send more than 12,000 emails a month.

It's easy to use once you have created an account. Templates are available to easily put together newsletters, including an option to upload images and graphics.

Some businesses use it to send a newsletter out, weekly, fortnightly or monthly. The content might include details about new products or services, information about special offers or profiles of new members of staff.

Competitions and customer surveys can be publicised through the service as well.

There is an opportunity to segment your mailing list so you can target relevant subscribers with different mail-outs.

Mails can be sent immediately or scheduled for a later date.

Each new email is called a campaign and once it has gone out to your database you will get statistics on how many people clicked on the email to view the content and the proportion of subscribers who clicked on particular online links.

This is important because you will see what interests the people who receive the emails so you can tailor it for future campaigns.

It's a good way of driving traffic to your website and inviting relevant individuals and organisations to connect with you on social media.

I will outline how you create an account in a moment but once it is set up you will need to create the all-important email contact list.

This can be done manually (using cut and paste from your email contacts), it can also be uploaded from a spreadsheet or, alternatively, imported from your Customer Relationship Management (CRM) list.

You have the option to create a sign-up form which can be posted on your business website or Facebook page for subscribers to indicate they want to receive your newsletter campaigns.

How to create a MailChimp account:

- Go online to www.mailchimp.com
- Click 'Sign Up Free' at the top of the page
- Fill in your business email, a username and password when prompted
- Click 'Get Started'

Alternatives to MailChimp, which also have a free option, include:

SendinBlue : www.sendinblue.com
Zoho Campaigns : www.zoho.com

27

RESPOND PROMPTLY & APPROPRIATELY TO ANY SOCIAL MEDIA POSTS OR COMMENTS

This is a reactive, rather than proactive, method of promoting your business and care should be taken with it.

It goes without saying that you need to monitor your social media platforms at regular intervals.

Lots of the feedback might be positive, in the form of retweets and 'likes' on Twitter or comments on one of your Facebook or You Tube posts.

This is all great third-party endorsement of your business and you need to let the world know that others like what you are doing.

Reply to the comments by thanking them, which will also show off the human side of your company.

You may even want to spark further discussion with your social media followers by expanding a debate and drawing others into it.

Making a connection with people in this way makes it far more likely that they will want to do business with you, either immediately or in future.

Monitoring your social feeds may also unearth criticisms of your business and even the odd abusive comment from a disgruntled customer.

This is important feedback too since it gives you the chance to address an issue and win that customer's trust back so they will return to you.

Your replies to Facebook comments or Twitter messages should have a respectful tone where you show that you understand the individual's grievance or you explain truthfully why the problem was encountered.

Resist the temptation to get into an argument with them, however, if they are not satisfied with your response.

Remember, some of your customers will be following the dialogue and you could lose them too if you react aggressively or unreasonably.

If possible, take the conversation offline by offering them your email address or a telephone number so you can discuss the matter privately.

28

USE GOOD SEARCH ENGINE OPTIMISATION (SEO) PHRASES

As a small business owner, it is a strong possibility that you have created and designed your own website using one of the free platforms such as WordPress or Wix.

These resources make it fairly easy to build your own website and update the content on a regular basis.

The challenge remains, however, to get prospective customers and clients to visit your site.

And the best way of doing this is to improve the Search Engine Optimisation (SEO) of your website.

Many businesses still pay through the nose to employ the services of IT gurus to develop their SEO.

But a little knowledge can go a long way and there are two main things you should aim to do to begin diverting a steady stream of online traffic in the direction of your site:

Use specific words and phrases people are searching for online in your website copy and blog posts

This involves a visit to the *Google Keyword Planner* (see Number 24 earlier in this chapter), which will tell you the number of times a word or phrase has been used to search for content relevant to your business in the previous month.

Make a point of including these words and phrases in the copy on your web pages and your blog, if you write one.

Don't overuse them, however, as Google gets suspicious when the same phrases keep popping up on the same website. It could adversely affect your site's ranking on the search engine if you use them too many times.

Influence other organisations to link back to your website from theirs

The more 'back links', as this is called, the more influential your website will appear to Google. And that means you'll get a higher ranking and have a much bigger chance of customers and clients finding you in an online search.

There are certain 'back links' you should particularly aim for because Google looks more favourably on them due to their standing and trustworthiness.

These include academic institutions, professional bodies such as chartered institutes and the mainstream media.

To achieve this you could contact your old school or university to tell them about your business and ask if they would feature you on their website in an alumni section, if they have one. Include a link to your web address and you will get a very important SEO boost.

You could also offer to write a guest blog for the professional body you belong to, offering best practice advice or some other added value content, always remembering to add a link to your website in your piece. Guest blogging would also work well with media publications.

Lastly, post some work-related videos on your free You Tube channel. Google owns You Tube and it will prioritise its own assets in search rankings.

It will be fantastic for your SEO if you can establish a popular video coupled with a link to your website so visitors will visit your site via You Tube.

29

SET UP A GOOGLE ALERT FOR YOUR BUSINESS

This is a great little tool for finding out when your business is being mentioned online, whether that is by the media or by a customer or partner organisation.

By setting up alerts around particular words, names or phrases you will get an email with a link to an article, website posting or blog as soon as it goes up on the web.

It's very simple to use:

- Go online at www.google.co.uk/alerts and you will arrive at a page with a search box containing the request to 'Create an alert about…'.
- Then type in the name of your business or your own name if you are a sole trader.
- Each time you create an alert you can also click the 'show options' tab which allows you to filter the search and confirm how often you want email notifications sent to you.
- When you've entered the search words and selected the options another box will come up asking you to insert the email address you want alerts sent to.
- Click 'create alert' and you will begin to be notified about all online mentions of your business.
- This is particularly useful if you operate in a service industry or the hospitality sector because you will become aware of comments being made about you by customers and clients on social media or on rating sites such as TripAdvisor.

You will be in a position to respond to critical and negative content by contacting the aggrieved party to deal swiftly with their complaint.

It is also important to know which newspapers and magazines are writing about your business and, when it is favourable, you can share an online link to the article on your social media feeds.

You can create alerts for any number of things so it is worth setting others up relevant to your industry so you get to learn about developments or issues which might affect your business.

Feel free to create Google Alerts for your competitors too, whether they are local, regional or national, so you can monitor what they are up to.

This chapter will have given you plenty of ideas on using the internet to the advantage of your business.
Next up is a chapter on networking with other businesses and how you can work with them to significantly increase each other's customer bases.

CHAPTER 6

Network with other businesses

www.prforsmallbiz.com

30

MAKE CONNECTIONS ON SOCIAL MEDIA WITH THE LOCALS

If you are running a new accountancy start-up it might not initially make sense to make a connection on social media with a local hairdresser, for example.

But the advantage in doing this is you can start building a relationship with each other by sharing comments and posts on Facebook or Twitter which will eventually build a sense of trust between you.

The upshot is that the hairdresser may end up recommending your business to potential new customers.

By making lots of connections with local companies and organisations and taking the time to engage with them on social media you can develop a number of brand ambassadors (see Chapter 4) for your products and services.

Everyone in business understands the values of a referral network where third-parties effectively sing your praises for you.

Social media gives everyone the opportunity to grow their businesses by leveraging the power of word of mouth recommendations.

The best ways to engage with other local companies are to reply to their posts, retweet, share or 'like' them if they are promoting something and generally show a friendly interest in what they are doing.

Even if you don't actually engage with another local business much, the chances are that they will see your posts and still recommend you because of your prominent online profile.

Here are some tips on how to find the social media usernames of fellow local businesses:

- Look through local newspapers and lifestyle magazines for features and adverts involving businesses and organisations and make a note of their website addresses – when you go online to their site you will find a link to their social media accounts

- Do a search on Twitter and Facebook (use the search bar at the top of the page) for local businesses – just by typing in the name of your village, town or city will bring up a list of local accounts including businesses

- Have a look through the private and business phone directories and then look them up online

Follow as many as you can and you will find that a fair number will follow your company back on Twitter or 'like' you on Facebook.

When they follow you on Twitter, send them a Direct Message (private post which only you and the other party can see) thanking them for the follow and say you are looking forward to sharing tweets with them.

For those which don't immediately follow you back, it is worthwhile just sending them a tweet to say hello and wish them well in their business. You won't be able to Direct Message them until you both follow each other.

You should end with a sizeable boost to your following on Twitter and Facebook but make sure you then cultivate an online friendship with your new followers by sharing their posts and engaging with them on a regular basis.

31

JOIN IN WITH A REGULAR REGIONAL BUSINESS TWEET-UP

Businesses in most regions of the country hold a weekly 'Tweet-up session' which serves essentially as an online networking event.

The basic principle is that everyone uses a specified hashtag – for example, #Leicestershirehour or #ManchesterHour – and then posts relevant content on Twitter at the same time every week, usually for an hour between 8pm and 9pm.

If you make a point of taking part every week you can establish some useful connections with other business people, who might ultimately refer your goods and services to people in their customer base.

The most important thing to remember, though, is not to just post a barrage of promotional Tweets about your business.

This would be akin to attending a networking event in person and just giving out business flyers without talking to anyone.

The secret of online networking is to treat it like dating. If you talk about yourself all night your potential partner will get fed up and eventually ignore you.

That doesn't mean you shouldn't post anything which promotes your business or organisation. But the golden rule is to post promotional stuff just two or three times each time you take part in a business tweet-up.

Your other posts should be designed to engage with others and nurture relationships online.

Follow the timeline of Tweets and send a post to one of them – including the specific hashtag for the tweet-up - asking how their week has gone at work. You might also ask what their best-selling product is or the most popular service they offer.

Alternatively, ask what they have planned for the rest of the week.

Make a connection and they will respond. When they tweet a reply their followers will see it and become aware of your business, as well as others taking part that night.

One thing I would strongly advise you not to do is to schedule tweets during the tweet-up using a tool such as Hootsuite or TweetDeck.

If, for some reason, you can't take part on a given week then, by all means, schedule a single tweet at the start of the tweet-up to make your apologies for not being involved and wishing everyone well.

But don't schedule a series of tweets beforehand. Some people will attempt to engage with your tweets only to get nothing back. They may think you're ignoring them and it could damage any future relationship with them.

The whole point of online business networking using Twitter is to build bonds with other businesses by engaging with them and ultimately stimulating them to act as a brand ambassador for you in the region you operate in. Some of those you encounter may well become customers too.

32

ATTEND BUSINESS NETWORKING EVENTS

We've looked at ways of networking online but, of course, you can also do it the old fashioned way, face-to-face!

This involves more of a commitment, in terms of making time available at set times of the week or month and making the effort to travel if you live a distance from the venue.

But it will pay off. There are great benefits from actually talking to someone in the same room. You can build a level of trust with the other person, whether you develop a friendship with them or you just impress them with your professional authority.

Some of these networking groups can be expensive to join but, since this book is all about free ways of promoting your business, do an online search for free business network meet-ups.

And if there isn't one, think about starting one yourself. If you are a one-man or one-woman band you could join with others in the same position in your locality, with the bonus that it can be a social organisation for sole traders as well as a network group.

But even if you have a small business with a number of staff it is well worth networking face-to-face.

This is how a business network group will lead to more customers or clients:

1) **It will generate referrals for you** – people you meet will tell others about your business and their third-party endorsement of you will be very powerful.

2) **You will do business with other members** – some members may invest in your services and there will be opportunities to do joint-ventures or partner up with others if they are in a relevant profession.

3) **New connections will lead to new business leads** – by connecting with others there will be opportunities to tap into their customer bases.

4) **Best practice will be shared** – by giving advice to each other you will improve the way you run your business and the way you sell your products or services.

5) **You will raise your profile** – more people will know about you and what you have to offer so it follows that more are likely to invest in you.

Now, I realise that some of you reading this book might be shy and lacking in confidence to pitch up at a networking group and sell your business to others.

But there are certain things you can do to make it easier for yourself:

- Give out lots of business cards and ask for those of other members
- Smile and show you are approachable
- Go up to a person on their own or a small group and introduce yourself
- Listen to others – people love talking about themselves
- Ask to be introduced to other people relevant to your business

It's a fact that everyone who attends a business network group for the first time is nervous and invariably stressed about it. Remember that and follow the bullet points above and you will be fine. Once you have been a couple of times you will actually look forward to it!

33

PARTNER UP WITH OTHER BUSINESSES & AGENCIES YOU DO BUSINESS WITH

Earlier in this chapter we touched upon the benefits of creating social media connections with other businesses in your locality to act as brand ambassadors for each other and nurture opportunities for third party referrals.

Well, you can do something similar by partnering up with fellow business people and organisations you work with.

For a pub landlord, this might mean your food suppliers, the brewery you take deliveries from and a staff agency which places employees with you.

In the case of a physiotherapist, this would involve sports clubs you work with, hospitals and health clinics which refer patients to you and suppliers of medical products or exercise equipment.

Or for a builder, this would refer to other tradesmen you work alongside on jobs, estate agents, developers and builders' merchants.

Whatever industry or profession you work in, there will be this network of businesses which rely on each other.

And because of this shared history and trust they are in a position to vouch for each other when it comes to recommending their services.
So why not take advantage of this by maintaining a relationship with them via social media.

Even if you've worked with another company only once and are unlikely to do so again make sure you link up with them on Twitter, Facebook or an appropriate social channel.

The chances are that you will have between five and 10 other businesses in your own personal network which either supplies you, buys from you or partners with you to deliver a service or product.

Sing each other's praises on social media because third party promotion is so much more powerful than shouting about yourself.

We've seen how important it can be to network with other businesses.
In the next chapter I will focus on two important social media platforms – Facebook and You Tube – and show how you can use them to promote your business effectively.

CHAPTER 7

Get the most out of Facebook & You Tube

www.prforsmallbiz.com

34

CREATE A BUSINESS PAGE ON FACEBOOK

Many businesses use their Facebook page as their official website and it is easy to see why.

It's free to use and easy to update, as well as providing an engaging platform for you to interact with customers and clients.

There are some basic things you need to do to make sure your Facebook page benefits your business and here they are:

- Do not use your personal Facebook page – keep that for friends and family.

- You need to have a personal page but you can set up a business page linked to it – click on 'create page' on the column on the left of your page and then click on either 'Local Business or Place' or 'Company, Organization or Institution, whichever is relevant.

- Add a logo image and a landscape photo across the top of your page.

- Fill in the 'About' details, giving a precis of your company, address and contact details.

- Start posting content before you follow other customers/clients or businesses so others can see you have a busy page worth following when you do connect with them.

- Post content from your company website, if you have one, with appropriate online links to help drive traffic to it.

- Striking images and videos get the most shares on Facebook so make sure you post plenty of them to illustrate your work or the people you employ.

- Keep your posts relatively short to ensure people engage with them – if they are too long and rambling your audience will switch off and scroll down to the next post in their Facebook timeline.

- Make sure your content sparks two-way conversations by asking questions or challenging followers to give their views on particular issues – by drawing others in, your content will be seen by the friends of your friends on Facebook.

- Post content when the most of your audience is likely to be reading it – this will depend on your line of business but generally it is best to post at lunchtimes on weekdays because Facebook is checked by people at work and in the early evenings after people have had their dinner.

- Use a free tool like Hootsuite or TweetDeck to schedule posts each day at timely intervals – intersperse these with 'live' posts for events which are happening in real time or comments on topical issues occurring that day.

- After 30 people have 'liked' your page you will get access to Facebook 'page insights' – check these regularly to see the demographics of your audience, when your audience is actually on Facebook and to find out which of your posts get the most engagement with followers.

35

RUN A COMPETITION ON FACEBOOK

An excellent way of building your Facebook following as a business is to run a competition for customers.

You should stipulate that entries will only be accepted from those who 'like' your page in the first instance.

If the prize is sufficiently worthy then you are likely to get a good response.

And, remember, each time someone 'likes' your business page it will be seen on their timeline.

So their Facebook friends will see it and the mere act of liking your page will be seen as a third-party endorsement and, ultimately, a positive review of what you do.

Facebook offers a competition set-up template for you at https://apps.facebook.com/my-contests/ where you are asked to give your competition a name, create an entry form and set a question or questions.

You can, of course, opt to run your competition using the usual status update box.

This is a checklist of things to do every time you post a competition on Facebook:

- Stipulate that entrants must first 'like' your Facebook page
- Include a list of competition rules and a deadline for entries to be sent in by
- Use a nice relevant image to announce the competition (remember, photographs attract significantly higher engagement on social media than other content)
- Ask a question which is not too challenging, so you don't put too many off entering
- Preferably ask a question relevant to your business where the answer is contained on your website (this will drive traffic to your site)
- Check Facebook rules for competitions by referring to the following link www.facebook.com/page_guidelines.php (because the rules can change regularly)
- Promote the competition on your other social media channels

There are plenty of options when it comes to running a competition on Facebook.

Your main aim with them is to influence people to engage with the post and preferably share it with their friends.

Here are some possible competitions to think about:

- The best photograph of someone trying one of your products, using your services or having a meal or a drink in your pub or restaurant, for instance

- A question about something you do as a business

- A funny caption competition based on a photograph taken at your workplace

- Ask entrants which of your products/services they like the most and to explain why in a limited number of words

- Link in with a special event, such as Mother's Day or New Year's Day, and ask entrants to share a photograph of a relative or friend enjoying the occasion

- Post a photograph of a partially-visible object to do with your business and ask entrants to guess what it is

36

TARGET CUSTOMERS USING FACEBOOK ANALYTICS

So you are regularly posting on Facebook but how do you tell how effective your content is in terms of engaging your audience?

The answer is *Facebook Insights*. These are the statistics which tell you how many people are reading particular posts and the number of people who are engaging with them.

The beauty of this free tool is that you can easily find out which posts are popular with your followers and which are not.

It follows that you should repeat the style and content of those which work.

The insights analytics will also let you know when the majority of those in your locality are usually on Facebook so you know the best times to post.

The data will also reveal the level of engagement with your posts. This refers to the percentage of people who reacted to them in terms of sharing the content, clicking on it or commenting on it.

Insights also tells us how many people 'liked' a particular post and the reach of each one (the number of people who saw it).

So how do we use the information from Insights to engage with our Facebook following?
The first thing to do is to look back over posts during the previous month and make a note of those which attracted the biggest engagement.

Do they have something in common? For example, do most of them involve visual content such as photographs or videos. Or do the majority involve posts about special offers or a particular service or product?

Whatever the common feature is, make sure you repeat this in future posts.

And use the analytics to work out the best time for you to post, when you are likely to reach most of your followers. Lunchtimes are often a good time to post simply because people often look at their phones while they are eating or taking a break from the workplace.

Another important stat in Facebook Insights is the one showing the demographics of your followers.

This is particularly important if your business relies on a local customer base. If the demographics show that a high proportion of your following do not live locally then you need to start connecting with more local friends and likers.

And if your business offers products or services for predominantly male or female customers then you need to check that the Insights demographics reflect this on your Facebook page.

To access Facebook Insights, click on the 'Insights' tab at the top of your page.

This will reveal a page of overview stats relating to recent posts.

Down the left side of the Insights page you will see options for 'likes', 'reach', 'page views' and 'messages'.

There is also an option for 'people' which tells you the proportion of men and women who follow you, their ages and the country they live in.

The 'local' tab in Insights has the information about what time people in your locality were on Facebook during the previous month.

So if you have a business Facebook page make some time to view the Insights so your posts are as powerful and engaging as you can make them.

37

SET UP A YOU TUBE CHANNEL FOR YOUR BUSINESS

A fair number of small businesses I have worked with have told me they had never considered setting up their own You Tube channel until I suggested it.

Some feared it would be too expensive and others felt they lacked the nous to actually do it.

In fact, neither of those statements is actually true. Creating your own channel is free and it really is quite simple if you have basic knowledge of how a computer works.

Now consider three facts about You Tube:

- It is owned by Google so it stands to reason you will climb the online search rankings when you post videos on a You Tube page

- It has been found that videos are on average 53 more times likely to appear on the first page of Google searches than any other content

- The click-through-rate (CTR) – those who click on a specific link instead of merely viewing a web page – is 43 times higher with video than other content

We will consider what kind of videos you should be posting and the protocols you need to go through to influence people to see them in a moment.

But, first, we will go through the simple process of setting up your own You Tube channel.

Before starting, you need to set up a Google account, if you don't already have one.

Go to the Google home page, click 'sign in' at the top right and then 'create account', where you will be asked to fill in some personal details to set yourself up.

Then go to the You Tube page at www.youtube.com before doing the following:

- Click 'sign in' at the top right and enter your Google log-in details

- Click on 'My Channel' at the top left

- Click on 'use a business or other name'

- Choose a name for your new channel (something relating to your business) and then select a category from the dropdown menu

- Click 'done' and you will then see the set up for your channel

- You will now need to customise it for your business

- Add your company logo or a personal picture, if you are a sole trader, to where it says 'icon'

- Add a wide background image to where it says 'channel art' – this might be an attractive generic shot to showcase what you do or a nice shot of your premises

- Add a description for your business by clicking the 'About' link and click 'channel description'

- Describe your business as clearly as you can, outline the type of videos you will be posting and include some relevant keywords to help customers find you on online searches

- Add online links to your company website and other social media by going to the pen symbol on the right of your main 'channel art' background picture

- Click 'done' and you should then be able to see the links displayed to your website and social media accounts. Click them to test that they work

So, you now have a You Tube channel for your business. Let's now look at the type of videos you should be aiming to post there.

38

POST VIDEOS ON YOUR YOU TUBE CHANNEL SHOWCASING YOUR PROFESSIONAL PROWESS

I'm assuming you have a smartphone, as a business owner, and these are perfectly capable of shooting high quality films to post on your You Tube page. If you have a digital camcorder or camera which films video, or you can borrow one, then use that to film shoots.

As this is a new You Tube channel, you need to introduce yourself and describe the products or services you offer.

A good first video would be you talking to camera for no more than 90 seconds.

Write yourself a set of bullet points to cover who you are, background about you, the name of your business, what your business does, your previous experience in your industry and an invitation to subscribe to your channel to watch forthcoming videos.

Alternatively, you could get a colleague, friend or family member to interview you (they will be off camera), going through questions which will reveal the checklist bullet points you want to highlight for viewers.

Keep your videos brief – the attention span of someone online is notoriously short and if they see your video is five or 10 minutes long you will likely lose them a short way into it.

If you feel you need longer than 90 seconds to outline your business, shoot two or three so you can concentrate on different arms of the business or different services or products you want to highlight.

The nature of the content will differ from business to business but here are some generic suggestions which will work across You Tube channels in a variety of industries:

- *Showcase your professional prowess* – make a video of yourself making a coffee for a customer, preparing flowers for sale, selling a house, repairing a car, or whatever else you do in your business

- *Film a virtual tour of your business premises* – this shows customers and clients where you work and legitimates your company

- *Interview members of staff about what they do* – a video like this humanises your business and makes people more likely to want to do business with you

- *Interview satisfied customers or clients* – these act as powerful testimonials and online reviews – viewers can see these are real people who have benefited from your products or services

- *Introduce new members of staff* – ask them what they hope to bring to your company and what their level of expertise is, to further humanise what you do

Of course, merely posting a video on your You Tube channel will not automatically ensure people will see it.

There are certain things you need to do to make it visible and the main ones are:

1) Write good titles for your videos – they need to be short, descriptive and should contain keywords that people are searching for online

2) Include strong search engine optimisation (SEO) terms – You Tube is the second largest online search engine (beaten only by Google) so if you get this right you can attract a big audience. Pay attention to the keywords in the title of your site and the title of your videos and also include relevant tags

3) Share links to your videos on your other social media accounts,

such as Twitter, Facebook and LinkedIn – studies have shown that content with videos or photographs are shared and viewed significantly more than other content

4) Encourage comments on your videos by asking questions within the film and make sure you monitor comments so you can respond to them and keep an online conversation going

5) Include references to your You Tube channel on emails and any printed literature you give to customers/clients and remember to include a link to it on your other social media accounts

39

MAKE A FREE ANIMATED VIDEO TO POST ON SOCIAL MEDIA

It's a good idea to mix up the content on your social media feeds to keep followers interested.

That means posting videos and photographs as well as your regular content.

And I would also advocate putting together some short animated videos to illustrate your business.

I can already hear some readers dismissing this idea because it sounds like it needs a fair degree of technical expertise.

But this isn't the case at all. There are resources available which are very easy to use and the best thing is they are free.

I mentioned earlier in this chapter about how people are significantly more likely to engage with visual content than other social media posts.

And animated films also fall into this category. They act as a fun showcase for your products and services and something different from the other promotional content you might be posting.

There are a number of online resources which enable you to easily make animated films for your business without you having to pay anything for the privilege.

Some of the best are:
GoAnimate www.goanimate.com
Animaker www.animaker.com
Moovly www.moovly.com

These websites offer a selection of creative themes which allow you to select appropriate characters, backgrounds and props.
As we have already seen, short videos work best when you are attempting to retain the attention of your audience online and animated films are no different.

When you get a moment, have a go at creating a film. There is a simple walk-through process to help you put them together.

Post it on social media and see what kind of reaction you get. If it engages people and you think it is appropriate for your business then make some more.

Animated films work well when you want to showcase your professional skills in a more dynamic way. They are great for professionals such as accountants, financial consultants and lawyers where the job is mainly office-based and difficult to illustrate in other visual ways.

There are paid packages which allow you to do more with your animated films on all of these platforms but the free option is enough for you to be able to share them on your business Facebook and You Tube pages.

Now that we understand how to use Facebook and You Tube effectively, we will look next at how engaging with the community can hugely benefit your business.

CHAPTER 8

Get involved with your local community

www.prforsmallbiz.com

40

DO SOME PRO BONO OR CHARITY WORK

You may feel as a small business owner that all your time is devoted to making it a success, particularly if you are attempting to grow a new start-up.

But keep an eye out for any charitable activities in your area and offer to get involved if your professional skills are relevant.

For example, an accountant could volunteer their expertise to help a charity balance its books for a fundraising project.

A public relations or marketing company might put themselves forward to promote an event for a good cause while a restaurateur could make their chef available to help with the catering for a project.

Ultimately it will reflect well on your business and your brand, as well as doing something good for the community.

Your enterprise might get a mention in a local newspaper or magazine.

And you can throw your support behind the charity or event by posting about it on your social media channels.

Huge businesses are doing something similar under the banner of what has come to be known as 'corporate social responsibility'.

They know it is important to be shown to be operating ethically and conscientiously.

It also happens to be great PR which is why small businesses should also aim to do it by getting involved in community projects and fundraisers.

It's important that you don't take any payment for this kind of work, not even sundry expenses.

You may well enjoy getting involved in charity work and eventually consider joining a local organisation such as a Rotary club or Round Table, where you will get the chance to mix and network with other business people and influential individuals in your community.

41

GIVE A TALK TO CHAMBER OF TRADE MEMBERS

This is particularly useful if your business relies on a local clientele.

It's worth becoming a member of your town or city's chamber of trade, purely because of the opportunities it presents to network and share information and best practice with other traders and business people.

But even if you are not a member it is well worth offering to do a talk at one of their monthly meetings.

You could pick a topic which is likely to resonate with a broad section of members.

This might be something to do with a successful way you use social media to promote your business, a customer service innovation you are pioneering or advice on how to do your own accounts.

Another topic might be to talk about a challenge you have overcome within your business which is generic to other businesses.

You can always include little references about what you do and how successfully you do it so chamber members are likely to recommend you to other local people after they leave the meeting.

This third-party referral and word-of-mouth recommendation is incredibly powerful and is likely to secure you new business as a result.

Talking about your business is also great practice for when you come to selling yourself to potential clients and approaching cold leads.

You will be surprised how much you have to offer other business people, in terms of passing on advice and best practice from your own experiences.

If you are lacking confidence in public speaking it can help to have a PowerPoint presentation on a screen so your audience has something else to concentrate on other than just you.

If you don't have access to a screen, make a list of bullet points to give your talk a structure.

Start by introducing yourself, your professional background and a brief outline of your business.

After the main body of your talk it's a great idea to end by asking for questions from the audience.

42

ATTEND SCHOOL & COLLEGE CAREERS EVENTS

There are many advantages of attending careers fairs at schools and colleges.

For just a couple of hours of your time you will come into contact with talented young people who may well be suited to your profession and may even become future employees.

If you engage with them and share your passion for the industry or trade you work in, it will encourage them to talk about your business to parents, grandparents, siblings and friends.

Some of these could well become customers or clients as a result of this.

Go there with the intention of offering work experience or internships to any of the youngsters who show a real interest in the work you do.

Approach teachers or lecturers and offer to give a careers talk to students to further promote what you do.

Remember, this is a two-way process. You are gaining publicity for your business but you're also offering a very personal first-hand insight into working in your particular field.

Take lots of business cards too and invite interested students to visit your workplace if they want to know more about what goes on there.

Hopefully, the educational establishment you visit will feature a reference to your visit on their website and an online link to your business.

And, as I have touched on elsewhere in this book, Google looks very favourably on back links from schools and colleges and this is reflected in strong rankings in any online searches.

43

APPROACH STUDENTS TO DESIGN A NEW BUSINESS LOGO FOR YOU

You might be thinking of sprucing up the image of your business and one way of doing it is to rethink the look of your brand.

A dynamic new logo could do wonders for you. And you don't need to spend any money getting a redesign.

There is a fair chance your local further education college or a local school has a graphic design course so why not approach teachers or lecturers to see if they would be interested in taking it on as a class test.

The benefits of this are that:

- The students gain from being challenged to do real work experience
- You gain from having talented students offer you a variety of new logo designs to choose from

- The winning design can also be promoted in a press release to showcase the winning student's talents, the quality of the course and your business will also get a mention

- The school or college may well post an article about the competition on their website and because Google strongly values back links from an educational site it will rank high in online searches

This idea doesn't have to be restricted to logo redesigns.

You could approach fashion students to create a new look for staff uniforms or IT students to write fresh copy for your website.

Don't feel shy about going to colleges and schools to enlist help with work like this. As I mentioned above, it will be valuable for the students to gain experience in projects which have a real life significance.

44

SUPPORT A LOCAL ISSUE

If your business has a local customer base and you feel particularly passionate about an issue which affects the community then feel free to get involved.

I don't mean 'piggybacking' on something in order to sell more products and services.

It is important that you have a passion for the cause or it would be disingenuous to throw your weight behind it.

It would also be ethically wrong to try to profit on the back of it.

But there is nothing to stop you offering to help with a campaign, by serving on an action committee and helping with distributing posters or leaflets and displaying them at your business premises.

What you will get from this is an elevation of your professional profile and a boost to your reputation as a caring community organisation.

Issues this might work with include the following:

- A battle to save the maternity or A&E unit at the local hospital
- Calls for a pedestrian crossing to improve road safety
- A campaign to retain the local Post Office in a central location
- A fight by parents to prevent a school being closed
- An initiative to prevent a popular pub being converted into housing

The element all these have in common is their perceived importance to a community.

You would be on safe ground supporting any of the above since it is highly likely that most of the local population would back them too.

If you are also vocal in the press about this type of issue then people will identify you as a caring individual or organisation.

And, consequently, one which can be trusted when it comes to doing business.

I would advise against getting prominently involved in contentious issues.

In that instance, you would likely alienate some existing and prospective customers. For the same reason, you are better off steering clear of anything with a political slant.

We've just seen the huge advantages of getting involved with your local community as a business and now it is time to look at one of the best ways of raising your profile online, through writing blogs.

CHAPTER 9

Write regular blogs

www.prforsmallbiz.com

45

WRITE A BLOG EVERY WEEK OR TWO WEEKS

This is a great way of letting people know about your expertise in a certain area.

Anyone can start a blog for free and begin posting their thoughts online on a regular basis.

The trick is to produce interesting content which will entice readers to subscribe to your blog so they continue to receive them via email.

Blogs written just to promote your business will not work. It is a waste of time to use them to say how wonderful your products or your services are.

Instead you would be better advised to write about developments in the industry you work in or personal stuff to do with yourself or your employees and their unusual hobbies or their charity fundraising efforts.

Make them interesting and people will read them and come back for your next one.

You can still mention your business but make it subtle, perhaps when you sign off the blog at the bottom. There might, of course, also be a reference to the company in the name of your blog.

And when you have posted a new blog make sure you let people know through social media or alerts on your website.

Ask people to comment on it because the more people who engage with your blogs, the more visible it will be on online searches.

If you are stuck for ideas for blog subjects, here are a few to get you going:

- New laws affecting your industry
- A topical local or national news story relevant to your business

- A charity fundraising effort by yourself or an employee

- A member of staff's unusual hobby

- A case study about a customer or client and how you have helped them

- Photographs from a special event

There are several platforms which allow you to set up a business blog. The most popular are probably the following:

WordPress www.wordpress.com
Blogger www.blogger.com
TypePad www.typepad.com
Tumblr www.tumblr.com

I always recommend to clients that they use *WordPress* because it gives businesses so many options to customise their blog.

It can also act as your business website because the free platform allows you to set up multiple pages from a drop down menu.

To set up a *WordPress* blog go through the following steps:

- Go to www.wordpress.com and click 'Create Website'

- You will then see a list of subjects and you will need to click 'Business & Services'

- Another list will appear with categories for different businesses

- Click the most appropriate one and you will be shown a selection of templates to choose from for your blog

- Click one of these and you will be directed to select from a number of different themes

- Once you've selected one of these you will be asked for a domain name for your site

- Choose one which will enable customers to find you easily (free

WordPress blogs will all end with .wordpress.com)

- You will see if your choice is available or similar options which are available

- Make a selection and then take the free option to create your blog site

- WordPress will then walk you through the process of customising your blog with business information and images and how to post blogs

To help you write blogs which are engaging and likely to be shared on social media, I have provided samples of great business blogs which can act as templates for your posts, in the 'Extra Resources' chapter at the end of this book.

46

POST COMMENTS ON RELEVANT BLOGS ABOUT YOUR PROFESSION

As well as writing regular blog posts for your business you should endeavour to connect with other bloggers writing about your industry or about issues in the area you work in.

Search for other relevant bloggers online and subscribe to their posts so you are notified by email each time they write something new.

And then spend 15 or 20 minutes every now and then writing a comment at the bottom of blogs when they have a specific relevance to your business and where you can contribute to the debate and add something valuable.

This will quickly establish a connection with other bloggers and make them aware of your business and your blog too.

It takes time to develop an audience for a blog. A large number attract no comments at all. And this is due to a lack of engagement by the writer. There are so many new posts online that you have to fight to get your share of the audience.

Sometimes it is enough just to write a short sharp comment such as 'great blog, thanks for sharing' just to show you appreciate the content.

Another comment might ask a question of the author, perhaps, to elaborate on their post or to expand the argument.

On occasions, you may wish to take an alternative view to what has been written.

But just by engaging with other bloggers will make you and your business more visible to potential customers and increase your relevance within the industry online.

47

ENGAGE WITH BLOGGERS WHO WRITE ABOUT YOUR INDUSTRY

One effective way of raising your profile as a business is to engage with bloggers who write about your industry.

Target those who have healthy followings online and who are seen as influential voices of authority.

This works particularly well in the business to business (B2B) sector where a high-profile third-party endorsement can lead to you landing lots of new leads and customers.

By the same token, if you've got a new product you want to publicise, ask a blogger to review it in the hope that they will become brand ambassadors for you.

I work with a client in the education sector and, in the course of developing their PR strategy, I suggested engaging with so-called 'mummy bloggers'.

We got dozens of parents, and their children, trying out the educational resource my client was offering and then blogging about it.

The vast majority have been very positive endorsements for the resource and, of course, they then share their blogs on social media where their followers are mainly other parents who also then take an interest in it.

Aside from the online traffic generated by the blogs, my client was also able to create a new tab on their website to showcase the many positive reviews from mummy bloggers. These are real people and carry much more weight than testimonials, which are often little more than a couple of lines under someone's name.

So, I hear you ask, how do I go about finding the important bloggers relevant to my business?

Try the following:

- Do a search on Twitter using appropriate key words, such as 'education blog', 'restaurant blog' or 'retail blog', depending on the nature of your business. Click on their profiles and you will probably see a link to their blog, which also doubles as their website. Also take a look at the people you already follow on Twitter because there may already be some influential bloggers in there.

- Read a trade publication specific to your industry and you will often see bloggers writing columns or articles in them. Editors of these publications will also often blog and it is well worthwhile engaging with these individuals.

- Speakers at industry shows are invariably important bloggers within the trade. So make a list of keynote speakers at the events you attend and then check if they write regular blogs which you can engage with.

- There are also dedicated websites which list key bloggers in different sectors and industries. One of these is www.bloggeries.com where you should find many of the blogs you need to be following and engaging with.

Of course, there is no such thing as a free lunch, as the saying goes. When you approach a blogger they will want something back from you if they are to entertain any thoughts of including your business in their latest blog.

This doesn't mean paying them. It's all about offering them interesting content, which will appeal to their readers.

So you could offer to do a guest blog for them about an interesting aspect of your business. Alternatively, why not offer them an interview so they can reproduce it in a Q&A (question and answer) format, which is always popular with bloggers and their readers.

Another way of getting the attention of a blogger is to give them a case study, describing how you helped a particular customer by supplying your products or services.

And if they do write about your business make sure you share links to the piece on your various social media accounts. This is very good third-party endorsement which will impress current and prospective clients and customers.

Now that we have examined the value of blogging and engaging with influential bloggers, it is time to look at three social media platforms which can be very effective for business people, namely LinkedIn, Instagram and Pinterest.

CHAPTER 10

LinkedIn, Instagram & Pinterest

www.prforsmallbiz.com

48

OPEN A LINKEDIN ACCOUNT & OPTIMISE YOUR PROFILE

If you are a business owner or a serious professional at any level it is in your best interests to have a LinkedIn profile.

It's the digital equivalent of a business card and gives you the opportunity to connect with others from the same industry, customers, clients and those you would like to do business with.

Your connections are able to easily access your business experience and professional qualities and you can see theirs.

The process of setting up a LinkedIn account, if you don't already have one, is simple:

- Go to www.linkedin.com and fill in your name, email address and a password where you are prompted to and click 'Join now'
- You will be asked to 'confirm your email address' to prove your identity
- Upload a professional-looking head and shoulders picture of yourself
- Edit your profile by typing in your company name and a description of the work you do
- Fill in details about previous employment
- Add a summary detailing what you do
- Add your specialities if you have particular professional skills
- Add as many connections as you can from your email address book or search for others from previous workplaces (the free part of LinkedIn only allows you to connect with someone if you have an email address for them)
- Include links to your business website, blog and social media

accounts

- Add relevant applications where you are prompted to do so, such as volunteering experience, awards or courses you have taken

Once you've set your account up and made some connections you should spend a little time optimising it to give yourself the best possible profile.

A few simple changes will make a real difference and entice potential customers and clients to make contact with you because they will see you as a reputable professional and a strong presence in your industry.

The following tips will help you optimise your LinkedIn account:

- Make sure you have a good high-resolution professional-looking profile photo – if you're not happy with the one you've uploaded, get a new one taken because first impressions are important in business

- Put in a clear, concise job title and steer clear of industry jargon

- Include your biggest professional achievements in the 'summary' section but keep it short. Add a few keywords relevant to your industry to help others search for your profile

- Also in the summary, upload a short video where you talk about your business and professional capabilities

- You might also want to upload a PowerPoint presentation to your summary through the 'presentation' symbol

- Fill in as many sections as you can, including periods of voluntary work and professional and academic qualifications

- Ask for recommendations from your connections because this will legitimise what you do and your professional qualities (a good tip is to recommend a few of your connections and they will return the favour)

- Keep your profile fresh by sharing relevant industry or business content in the 'share an update' box or write a short article in the 'write an article' section if you want to highlight something related to the work you do

- Connect with alumni from your old schools and colleges/universities because that shared study history can often help to cement a business connection quicker than if you haven't got that in common (under the tab 'My Network', select 'Find alumni' from the drop down menu and do a search)

49

CREATE A BUSINESS PAGE ON YOUR LINKEDIN ACCOUNT

You will be aware that LinkedIn is the world's major professional social networking site and it works effectively for individuals who want to showcase their expertise and qualifications.

But it is also well worth adding a business page to your personal profile to help make more people aware of your brand.

If you've not got one set up yet, simply go to the 'Interests' tab at the top and click on 'companies'.

On the right hand side you will then see a link for 'Create a Company Page' which will lead you to the set up procedure for your business page.

You can include a review of your business and a link to your company website if you have one.

If you have different, distinct elements to your business you have the facility to create a second business page, called a 'Showcase Page'.

These are designed to help build long-term connections with LinkedIn members who are more interested in a specific aspect of your organisation.

So if you are a manufacturing company but you export to the United States you might want to create a 'Showcase Page' dedicated to that side of your operations.

You might be a dental practice which also offers private cosmetic treatment and you decide to create a page for those services to differentiate from what you do for NHS patients.

A landscape gardener could set up a showcase page for the work he or she does on patios, for example, and a hairdresser has the option of focusing their wedding services on a showcase page.

Once your business pages have gone live, you need to keep them busy by posting regular relevant, engaging content, as you would do with any other social media platform.

When you are trying to build connections for your business page or pages you can share the posts from those on your personal LinkedIn page so your existing professional connections get to see them and, perhaps, decide to connect with the business pages too.

These business pages are all visible online and can give your business further valuable exposure.

To set up a 'Showcase Page':

- Log in to your LinkedIn company page
- Hover or click on the down-pointing arrow next to 'Edit' at the top of the page
- Select 'Create a Showcase Page' from the dropdown menu
- Give it a Showcase Page Name & click 'create page'

50

JOIN RELEVANT DISCUSSION GROUPS ON LINKEDIN

This is a way of making your LinkedIn profile more active and, as a consequence, ensuring you and your business are more visible in your industry.

Use the search bar at the top of the page to look for relevant groups. These might include individuals and organisations in the same line of business as you or people or businesses who are potential clients or customers.

Look for groups which have plenty of members and which are active. You might like the sound of one particular group but then find out it has only a handful of members and no-one has posted in it for the previous six months.

Have a look at some of the discussion threads once you have joined a group and if anyone has posted recently on a specific one which takes your fancy then contribute a comment of your own.

If it is your first interaction in the group, let the other members know and give them a warm greeting at the beginning of your comment.

Don't spend your time on a LinkedIn group just posting promotional messages about your business because you will quickly be ignored.

Build a rapport and a sense of trust with people and, in time, these other individuals may well refer prospective customers or business leads to you.

It may well be that there are no relevant groups on LinkedIn so it might be time to start one yourself.

Anyone can launch a new group but you will need to drum up support for it. Let relevant connections know about your plans to set it up and look for other professionals in LinkedIn who might be interested. Connect with them first before inviting them to join your new group.

The value of online business networking cannot be underestimated and social media provides us with brilliant platforms to do it on. These networks can lead to third-party referrals and genuine leads which are essential to help grow a small business.

51

OPEN AN INSTAGRAM ACCOUNT & POST PHOTOS RELEVANT TO YOUR BUSINESS

Instagram, where users essentially share images, is one of the fastest growing social media sites.

Latest figures show more than 400 million people post on it every month, including more than a quarter of the population of the United States and an estimated 14 million UK residents.

There are now more social networkers on Instagram than on Twitter, which will surprise some people.

So it is well worth starting an account if you don't have one for your business.

Obviously, some businesses will be more suited to posting online photographs than others.

But if you run an enterprise which relies on an interaction between your employees and customers or clients then there should be plenty of scope to use Instagram.

A pub licensee could post a photo of a pint of a new beer they have started selling on tap or a picture of a meal which has been prepared in the kitchen.

Shopkeepers might want to put up an image of themselves showing off a new product in stock while a travel agent could post a photo of an exotic location where a customer has just booked to go on holiday.

One of the most important things to do with Instagram pictures is to include lots of relevant hashtags to increase the searchability of the image.

So the holiday photo mentioned above could include hashtags such as #dreamholiday #holidays #holidayideas #vacations #exoticlocations and also a few references to which country it is in and the region.

A car garage could choose to showcase the skills of its employees by posting Instagram images, before and after, of repairs to the scratched bodywork of a car or a valeted vehicle.

As with Twitter, you need to engage with other businesses in your community, if you run a local business, and ask them to share your Instagram posts with their followers.

Instagram is another way you can easily build brand advocates for your business through others who reinforce the quality of the products or services you offer by sharing information online.

52

SET UP A PINTEREST PAGE & BUILD RELEVANT CONNECTIONS

Pinterest is a social media platform which enables users to create an online notice board containing content they are interested in.

As well as saving articles, blogs, images and videos to their own board they can also share it with other users.

It's true to say that almost all social media platforms are more useful for some businesses as opposed to others and this is certainly the case with Pinterest.

It's important to note that around seven out of 10 of its more than 100 million users are women so it follows that businesses which have predominantly female customers will benefit from being on it.

Health and fitness instructors, hairdressers, beauty therapy salons, spas, fashion labels, clothes shops and interior design companies use Pinterest well.

But it is also great for hospitality businesses, retail shops, sports clubs, theatres, cinemas and artistic professionals such as painters and sculptors.

Recent figures show that 40 per cent of users have discovered a product or service through Pinterest and pinned it to their board.

To set up your own business Pinterest account, follow these steps:

- Go to www.pinterest.com/business/create and fill in name, email address and a password

- Enter your business category from the dropdown menu

- Search for the subjects relevant to your business on the next page

- Add the Pinterest 'browser button' when prompted – this will make it easier for you to save content to your page

- You will then get a page up which tells you exactly how to save content to your page

Now it is time to start making your Pinterest page look great and making connections with other relevant users, customers, prospective customers and colleagues in your profession.

Here are some tips to do just that:

- Add your business name, your website and links to your social media accounts to make the page visible

- Post images showcasing your products or services and add a link to your website and your business/brand name each time you do it

- Post content from your website

- Pin interesting articles and great images relevant to your business

- Add the 'pin it' button to your website so others can save content about your products and services to their Pinterest boards

- Make sure you categorise the content you pin under the right category to make it easier for other users to find it

- Give other users tips on how to do certain skills, such as making a great cup of coffee if you are a barista, arranging flowers if you are a florist or doing stretching exercises if you are a fitness instructor (three-quarters of users say Pinterest is the best source of finding new interests)

- Create a special pin board on your page for customer reviews and testimonials

- Encourage staff members to contribute to the company Pinterest page by pinning content they find interesting and which is relevant to your business

- Pin content about new employees and fundraising/charity events your business has got involved in to show the human side of what you do

- Monitor your 'Pinterest Analytics' to see what other users like about your page and which content they save. You will get a pointer on the audience for your page. Look at which content is popular and make sure you post more of it

Hopefully this chapter has inspired you to set up, or develop existing, business LinkedIn, Instagram and Pinterest pages.
We've already looked in depth at Twitter, Facebook and You Tube and the next chapter will help you post engaging content on all of these platforms by outlining some social media best practice.

CHAPTER 11

Social media best practice

www.prforsmallbiz.com

53

POST A PHOTOGRAPH OR VIDEO ON TWITTER OR FACEBOOK

Research shows that content posted on social media with a relevant photo or video is much more likely to be viewed and shared than a post without.

For this reason it is worthwhile regularly adding a suitable picture with your online postings and, when you can, to post the occasional video.

It is important that videos are brief because the attention span of social networkers is notoriously short. 90 seconds is the maximum length of any film you should post.

As with Instagram, there are some businesses which lend themselves to sharing images of their operations and others which don't.

If you are selling products or services or dealing with people in your everyday working life then the chances are that there are plenty of opportunities to shoot photos and films and post them online.

Be aware of respecting the privacy of staff or customers, of course, and always ask if they mind featuring in an image or video to be posted online.

And take care that you don't have any children in the background as there are strict laws protecting young people appearing in images which are for public use.

There are numerous ways businesses can showcase their capabilities through pictures and films.

A hairdresser showing off a new hairstyle, a builder laying the final brick on a new housing development, a barista making the perfect cup of coffee, a landscape gardener capturing their latest piece of work, and so on.

More people are likely to see your tweet or Facebook post because of the attached photo or video and if they are interesting enough then they will be shared widely online, giving your business valuable exposure.

54

FOLLOW RIVAL BUSINESSES ON SOCIAL MEDIA

This is something business people are sometimes reluctant to do.

They worry that rivals will see what they are doing and attempt to compete with them.

But in the modern world where we share so much online with friends and colleagues there is no way of keeping your business practices a secret from competitors.

So, it makes perfect sense to keep an eye on what your rivals are up to.

Follow them on Twitter, Instagram and You Tube and 'like' their Facebook pages.

You will regularly pick up tips on how to improve your own social media profiles by spotting what others are doing in your industry.

Don't be afraid to copy an idea if you can see it is successful for a rival business.

For example, if a competitor has sparked a series of engaging comments and 'likes' after posting a photograph of a new product on Twitter or asking a question on Facebook then try it yourself.

Similarly, if you are thinking of posting something new like offering competition prizes or special offers via social media then have a look at your rivals to see if they've tried it and how successful it was.

Following local rivals on Twitter and Facebook can also result in a beneficial symbiotic relationship for both parties.

I know of businesses which have referred a customer to a competitor when they could not fulfil an order or service for some reason. The chances are that the rival business will return the compliment at some stage in the future.

If your business relies on a local customer base then make sure you search for other similar enterprises across the country.

This is a great way of sharing expertise and best practice with others in the same line of work.

Copy what they do well and don't be afraid to ask them how a particular social media campaign went for them so you can get a real insight into how successful it might be for you.

Social media allows small businesses to set up really useful networks of like-minded entrepreneurs and business owners but so many miss out on the chance to do it.

One of the most important things to note about social media is that it's more important for a business to have a relevant following than a huge following.

I worked with a client recently who had nearly 20,000 followers on Twitter. But once I delved into the analytics it transpired that roughly two-thirds of these people were not relevant. They weren't potential customers or individuals and organisations which could raise the client's profile.

In simple terms, every time that client had tweeted it was only interesting one-third of the audience.

So I would advise businesses to follow back only those followers which are relevant to your business. There is no need to build up a vast following because the use of hashtags and the influencing of others to share your content will ensure your posts still get seen by a wide online audience.

55

POST ONLINE LINKS FOR ANY PRESS COVERAGE YOU GET ON SOCIAL MEDIA

You will understandably be jubilant when you get an article or feature published in a newspaper or magazine.

But don't rest on your laurels thinking your job is done. It's great that print and online readers of that publication will see the piece.

But you want it to be seen across a much bigger audience so it reaches as many prospective customers as possible.

The best way to do this is through your various social media channels. Don't forget, this article is great publicity for your brand. Particularly, if it is an editorial piece which isn't seen as part of a paid-for advertisement.

As soon as the article appears you need to shout about it and influence others to share it for you too.

These are the things you must do when you post on social media about press coverage to ensure the piece is seen by a big audience online:

1) Reduce the length of the URL address for Twitter posts

You only have 140 characters so cut back the URL link to around 24 characters by using a free service such as the *Google URL shortener*. This will give you more words to play with.
It allows you to get more content in to explain what the article is about.
A recent change by Twitter means that photos do not take up any of your allocated 140 characters so all the more reason to include one to illustrate the press article you've featured in.

2) Use hashtags effectively

Hashtags, as I have explained earlier in the book, are the best way of getting your posts seen by many more people than those who follow you on social media. This applies specifically to Twitter and Instagram.
Use hashtags which contain words people are searching for on Twitter (see Number 13 for tips on this).

3) Show how pleased you are with the coverage

Phrase the post in such a way which shows how excited your business is to have an article published about it. This will influence others in the community to share it with their followers on their social media accounts.

4) <u>Include the Twitter, Facebook or Instagram handle/username of the newspaper or magazine in your post</u>

Media organisations which run the piece will be notified if you mention them in the post and they may choose to share your post on their social media. A good tip here is to thank the publication on Twitter or Facebook which will likely entice them to reply to you, giving your brand more exposure to their followers. Some of these could be customers as well, of course.

5) <u>Look for the post on the Twitter or Facebook pages of the publication</u>

If you spot a post about the article on the local newspaper's Twitter page, for example, make sure you retweet it. Share it on Facebook if you see it on your timeline there as well.
These are great endorsements for your business so you need to make sure everyone who follows you on social media gets to see that you are making a buzz in the media.

6) <u>Ask customers and friends to share the coverage with their social followers</u>

Don't be afraid to ask customers to share links to the article on their Twitter and Facebook pages. They are not likely to mind, especially if they have used your products or services over a period of time. These are all powerful third-party brand ambassadors for you. Get as many to share the press article as possible because they are effectively recommending your business to their family and friends.

56

SCHEDULE SOCIAL MEDIA POSTS USING FREE TOOLS SUCH AS HOOTSUITE

If you run a small business you are going to be short of time.

And this means you also have limited opportunities to post content on your various social media feeds.

For some, this means sending out five or six tweets one after the other or two or three Facebook posts a few minutes apart.

At best, this looks unprofessional and at worst you will alienate your audience, who will get fed up of seeing your posts clogging up their timelines.

Eventually, people will start to unfollow you if it continues to happen.

The solution to all of this is to get a free account with a social media management tool, such as *Hootsuite*, *Buffer* or *TweetDeck*, which allows you to schedule your posts at different intervals of the day, week and month.

I have always used Hootsuite and would recommend you start out on this platform because it is relatively easy to use.

It's a brilliant tool because you can actually sit down when you get an hour or two spare and post all of your content for the week on multiple social media accounts so that it appears at whatever time of the day you choose.

Hootsuite allows you to schedule posts for free on three social media accounts from Twitter, Facebook, Google+, LinkedIn, WordPress, Instagram and YouTube.

To set yourself up on Hootsuite do the following:

- Log on at www.hootsuite.com
- Sign up in the top right corner
- On the dashboard, add your three social networks by going to 'streams' on the left column and clicking 'add social network' at the top
- A box will then come up for you to choose a social media channel and then click 'connect with (the social media account)' where you will then be asked to enter your login details for that account so it

can be connected with Hootsuite

- You can then add streams for each social media account, such as 'timeline', 'my tweets', 'mentions' and 'scheduled posts' so you can monitor all the activity on your Twitter, Facebook or whichever social platforms you have

- To add streams, select 'streams' from the left hand column menu, click 'add tab' (a + sign at the top left), give it a name and press 'enter'

- Inside each tab, click 'add stream', then select a social network from the list on the left and choose a profile from the drop-down list before clicking on the streams you want to add for that profile

- You can then start scheduling messages by selecting the profile you want to post from at the top left and writing your content where it says 'compose message'

- At the bottom of the 'compose message' box you will see options to 'attach media' (photos or videos) and 'scheduling' where you choose when the post is to be published

- Posts can be edited at any time so if you make a mistake on the date for publication, or the details of the content have changed, then go back to your stream for 'scheduled posts' and click where it says 'edit'

- It's also worthwhile downloading the Hootsuite app on your mobile phone or tablet computer, as well as your desktop computer, so you can manage your posts wherever you are

I would add one note of caution, however. Don't rely on just scheduling your posts in advance because your social media accounts will appear automated to followers and that can be a negative vibe to give off.

When you get a moment, monitor your various social media feeds and reply and engage with other people.

Continue to post in 'real time' as well so you humanise your social media profiles.

Scheduling posts allows you to publish content at intervals but engagement with others throughout the day is still vitally important.

So you should be in a great position to use the power of social media to raise your profile online and, most importantly, to secure lots of new customers and clients.

To finish, I thought it was worth having a chapter devoted to thinking outside the box with a collection of miscellaneous ideas to help promote your business further.

CHAPTER 12

Thinking outside the box

www.prforsmallbiz.com

57

'PIGGYBACK' ON A TOPICAL ISSUE

It's a good idea when you start a business or when you are running a small business to keep abreast of topical issues.

Read newspapers – local, regional and national – to stay in touch with the news agenda.

These are stories which are interesting journalists so if you can find a link to one of them in your company or organisation then it follows that you stand a good chance of gaining press coverage.

This is particularly the case with your local newspaper, which will always be on the lookout for good stories to attract plenty of hits on their website.

If it's a topical issue, there is a much greater chance of this happening.

I would advise business owners to go through the papers once or twice a week and make a note of stories which have a relevance to the industry they operate in or the products or services they offer.

Here are some examples of how this might work:

Example 1:
A national story is hitting the headlines about a shortage of openings for NHS patients at UK dental practices.
- The manager of an NHS dental practice which has vacancies for patients could then 'piggyback' on this issue and send a press release out explaining they are bucking the national trend and new patients are welcome.

Example 2:
Newspapers are running the results of a survey which shows that 75 per cent of shoppers would prefer to eat food produced close to where they live.
- A coffee shop, delicatessen or restaurant might then decide to contact local journalists because they use mainly locally-sourced food and drink.

Example 3:

The new football season is about to kick off and the papers are full of previews of the new campaign.

- A sports shop could organise for a professional footballer or local semi-professional player to appear as the special guest for an open day – invitations can then be sent to the press with the offer of interviews with the player about the new season.

The beauty of all these initiatives is that businesses get free editorial coverage.

The subsequent articles don't even have to refer to any of the products or services being offered but they will serve to raise the profile of a start-up or SME and make many more potential customers or clients aware of them.

58

ENTER YOUR BUSINESS FOR AN AWARD

A great way to raise your profile is to put yourself forward for a relevant award or get someone to nominate you for one.

Most local newspapers run an annual business awards scheme and if you can get on the shortlist for one it will result in some great public relations.

The publication will run a profile of your company or organisation in the run-up to the presentation night which is great publicity even if you are not ultimately one of the winners.

Make a note, as well, of awards schemes run by relevant trade magazines.

Winning an award will result in a huge boost for your profile and an endorsement of the quality of your goods or services.

The press coverage will also do wonders for the Google ranking of your business and your online profile.

Make sure you share on social media any articles mentioning your business being nominated or winning an award and try to get others to do so too.

And if you are an award winner, flag it up on your website and include it on company stationery.

59

INCLUDE YOUR CONTACT DETAILS ON YOUR EMAIL SIGN-OFF

This may sound obvious but you would be surprised at the number of businesses I have dealt with where owners and managers fail to do this.

You should have the following information at the bottom of every business email you send out:

- Your name followed by abbreviations for any academic or professional qualifications
- Your business name and job title
- Email address
- Office landline telephone number
- Mobile phone number
- Social media links (usually Twitter & LinkedIn)
- Business website URL address

The big advantage of this is that you are effectively sending out your business card with every email you send.

If people don't have your contact details easily to hand like this they may well give their business to someone else.

If you have an IT person who has designed your website and set up your business email then it is a fair chance they will have added a sign-off like this.

But if you have signed up for your email address yourself then you might have overlooked doing it.

It is very easy to set up. Many businesses now use Google Gmail or Microsoft Outlook for their emails so I will show you how to set up a sign-off on each of those.

How to set up a Google Gmail sign-off

- Go to 'settings' (symbol which looks like a sun with rays coming out) at the top right
- Click on that and select 'settings' from the drop down menu
- Scroll down to the section marked 'signature' and click the box to say you want to enter one
- Fill in your contact details in the order indicated above
- Click 'save changes' at the bottom and you are done

How to set up a Microsoft Outlook email sign-off

- Go to the settings symbol (it also looks like a sun with rays coming out) at the top right
- Select 'options' from the drop down menu
- Under the heading 'Writing emails' select 'Formatting, font and signature'
- Enter your contact details in the order set out above in the box under the heading 'Personal signature'
- Click 'save' and you are done

60

OFFER CUSTOMERS A FREE 'NO OBLIGATION TO BUY' CONSULTATION

When you are offering a professional service to clients and customers it can be difficult if they've not used you before.

They might be able to see testimonials for your work on your website or they may have been referred to you by someone else but until you do some work for them they could well remain unconvinced.

One of the best ways to show that you are the solution to their business problem is to offer a free consultation.

This is essentially a foot in the door. A chance to show a potential customer you have the professional skills to help them.

I do this with my clients. I begin with a half-an-hour chat with them to find out what work they need doing, the timescale they want it delivered and the budget they have to work with.

Armed with all the information from the meeting, I will go away and put together a plan of action, outlining the current situation with the business I am helping, what they want to happen and how I am going to achieve it.

If you can show a good understanding of the business you are trying to help then you will have made a big step towards being taken on by the client.

So do your research on them. Go through every page of their website or company brochure, if you have access to one.

The key thing here, though, is not to give away ideas and plans which the prospective customer can then put into action without using your services.

In your plan of action, just outline the steps you will take without revealing detailed accounts of how you will do it.

Demonstrate an understanding of the challenges faced by the potential client and they will immediately warm to you.

Even if they don't take you on or they don't have the budget they may well recommend your services to others in their industry.

61

TAKE GOOD QUALITY STAFF MUG SHOTS WITH YOUR MOBILE PHONE OR DIGITAL CAMERA

If you have a website it will be improved immeasurably by having good quality photographs of yourself and members of staff.

Customers like to see who they are dealing with and if they see images of happy, smiling and professional-looking faces beaming back at them they are more likely to trust you and your business.

I have always encouraged business people to show the human side of their operation, whether it is through having engaging social media profiles or displaying friendly staff mug shots online.

There is every chance prospective customers and clients will check your business out on the internet before they approach you, particularly if they haven't used your products or services before.

You don't need to invest in a smart camera either. I am assuming you have a mobile phone and virtually all of these are now capable of taking crystal clear, high resolution photographs.

You might also consider using a point-and-shoot camera if you or one of your colleagues owns one.

Here are some basic photography tips to ensure your pictures stand out:

- A good tip is to take the staff pictures outside, where the natural light will give you a good image, assuming it is not too bright or it is tipping it down with rain.

- Pictures taken indoors can often be ruined by being taken in a dark environment or by the effects of artificial lighting. So take your subjects outside, if it is possible, and find a suitable background, such as a garden or a quiet street.

- Avoid brick walls and other dull surroundings and also steer clear of cluttered backdrops which contain lots of people and other distracting items.

- Aim to take head and shoulders pictures and keep them consistent (looking directly at the camera or turning slightly to the left or right, etc) to give them a uniform presence on your website.

- People often struggle to know what to do with their hands when they are being photographed. A good way to avoid this is to ask subjects to turn slightly, fold their arms and look towards the camera.

- Ask the subject to smile because you want them to look approachable when potential customers and clients log on to the page online.

You might also consider adding some personal details to each profile picture, such as a person's hobbies, something unusual they have accomplished or their favourite book or film.

This all goes towards humanising your staff and making them look more trustworthy as normal rounded individuals.

62

STAGE AN UNUSUAL STUNT

The challenge for many small businesses is to make themselves stand out from the crowd.

Most have a website and social media channels and these can both be very powerful promotional tools.

But what about staging an event which is out of the ordinary and which captures the imagination of people?

Your aim here is to organise something which the press will be interested in covering and which social networkers will rush to share with their online connections.

These are ideas which may well achieve this:

- Get a church choir or acapella group to sing outside your shop or office block (clearly, this works best if your premises is in a central location)

- Dress up staff as mascots reflecting the nature of your business

- Ask a street entertainer, such as a juggler or magician to perform outside your front door and involve customers

- Invite a local amateur dramatic society to stage an impromptu performance outside your premises

Word will spread when events like this are staged and onlookers will doubtless share videos and photos on social media.

The local media are also likely to descend on you but if they don't make sure you take your own pictures and videos so you can send them to the press and post on the likes of Twitter, Instagram and Facebook.

If you are feeling particularly adventurous it might be worth considering some so-called guerrilla marketing tactics.

This involves a sudden dramatic promotional event which is subtle but, ultimately, can be linked to your business.

Examples of this might be a dance troupe suddenly appearing outside your shop or office and putting on a dynamic performance before disappearing again.

This works well in a busy area such as a shopping mall or close to public transport terminals.

You don't need to spend any money on this. It can be organised by approaching a local dance or theatre group and asking them if they would like to promote an upcoming production by performing outside your business.

The mere fact the event takes place outside your business is enough for you to associate yourself with it. Subsequent mentions in the press and on social media will doubtless mention where it took place and give your company a name check.

This is more of a subtle way of promoting what you do but it all goes into helping to raise your profile and if it leads to just a handful of new customers or clients it is worthwhile doing.

63

PROMOTE YOURSELF ON THE BACK OF SPECIAL ANNUAL EVENTS

A great way of getting free media exposure is to link your business to a special day or week of the year.

You might be a florist offering something unusual to customers for Valentine's Day or Mothering Sunday.

Or a leisure centre putting on taster sessions in January at a time when more people commit themselves to getting fit.

Or you may be a pub which is having a special spooky makeover for Halloween night celebrations.

Another option is to plan ahead to time a news release around a special national awareness day such as National Smile Week, National Beer Day, Senior Citizens' Day or Read A Book Day.

There is a comprehensive list of these at www.awarenessdays.co.uk.

The media often runs articles to mark such occasions, particularly if they are quirky days.

And they will want a local link if they are a regional publication or a relevant business link if they are a trade title.

There may well be several of these days which you could link your business to so make a note of them and start thinking about newsworthy ideas you can hang a press release on.

Make sure you find out the copy deadlines for newspapers and magazines so you are able to send them releases in good time for them to be published in the issue closest to the special day or week you are connecting with.

64

TAKE GENERIC PHOTOS TO SHOWCASE YOUR BUSINESS ONLINE

Social media posts which include interesting photographs get 94 per cent more views than content unaccompanied by an image.

And this visual content is a whopping 40 times more likely to be shared online than other types of content.

Those statements alone should be enough to convince you to start snapping away and posting your pictures on the business Twitter, Facebook and Instagram accounts.

All smartphones now take fantastic quality photographs so there really is no excuse for not doing this.

You are probably already thinking of what images you need to post. Relevant photographic content will clearly be different from business to business but you need to be aiming to achieve the following with the pictures you post:

- Showcase the products/services you offer
- Raise the profile of your brand
- Portray yourself and key members of your workforce
- Highlight valued customers (if they agree, of course)
- Show off attractive elements of your office/factory/shop

You might decide to make a list of all the images you want to post and then set aside a couple of hours to go around the premises taking photographs.

This will give you a stockpile of pictures to post at regular intervals over the following weeks. This library of images will also come in handy when you send out press releases and you want to illustrate a facet of your business.

Other business people may prefer to take photographs as they get ideas for them. This more spontaneous method also works well, particularly if employees are pushed for time during the working day.

To give you inspiration for your business let's look at two fictitious businesses and how they might approach taking photographs for posting on social media.

1) Harry's Coffee Shop

- A close-up picture of one of the baristas pouring a coffee
- An employee holding a handful of coffee beans
- An image of one of the cakes which are sold
- A selfie of a staff member with a customer
- An exterior shot of the shop, if it has character

2) Aardvark Estate Agency

- An outside shot of a property you have just taken on for sale or rent
- An unusual feature inside the above property
- An image of a new member of staff at their desk
- If an employee is celebrating something in the office, snap them with a celebratory cream cake

When a property is sold take a picture of a member of staff taking away the sign outside

The reason that images are so popular on social media is simply that our brains process visual communications, such as pictures or videos, much quicker than a passage of text.

So if you really want to make a buzz online make sure you post plenty of pictures, using appropriate hashtags in the way I have already outlined in this book.

65

ASK TRADE MAGAZINES FOR A LIST OF THEIR FORTHCOMING FEATURES

Most small businesses think about advertising in trade magazines but often discount the idea on the grounds of cost.

But there is no reason why your business shouldn't feature in one of the key trade magazines which writes about your profession or the industry you work in.

Their journalists are always on the lookout for content which interests their readers and if you can come up with something suitable you've every chance of gaining some invaluable free editorial coverage.

I've already covered in this book advice on how to come up with good ideas for features and case studies.

But in this segment I will show you how to increase your chances of getting content published.

When you are pitching to magazines it is absolutely essential that you do so directly to the appropriate journalist. This might be the editor or someone who covers a particular aspect of your industry.

Their names should be on their website under the 'contact us' tab but if they aren't then don't worry about calling them to find out. They won't mind because journalists appreciate only relevant material being sent to them.

Keep in mind that most magazines work well in advance of their deadline so content needs to be submitted up to three months before the issue you want to be published in.

The good news is that most magazines have a 'forward features list', which essentially is a rundown of topics which will be covered in an upcoming publication.

You should be able to find this list on the website, usually under a tab labelled 'media' or 'advertise with us'. This should also contain a media kit which gives background information on the magazine, the demographic of its readership and the style of content it requires from contributors.

If you can't find the forward features list on the website then just give them a call and they will email you one.

Take a look at the upcoming features on the list and identify which ones you might be able to contribute to.

This might be a case study which illustrates an industry issue being highlighted in a feature, a quote or two from you, as an industry insider, on another topic or a feature relating to another article the magazine plans to run.

Remember that the content you supply should not be over-promotional. You are not advertising your business here.

The purpose of contributing to the feature is to help raise your profile and establish you as a voice of authority in your industry.

The magazine will mention your business in their article and that will be enough to make your brand highly visible to prospective customers and clients.

Of course, if you have taken my advice to cultivate relationships with journalists via social media then this whole process will be a lot easier.

When magazines are aware of you and your business through Twitter or Facebook, for example, then they are much more likely to want to use contributions from you in their features.

If you nurture a good enough social media relationship, journalists may well come to you for content or quotes without you even asking.

66

ENLIST THE HELP OF A CELEBRITY TO PROMOTE YOUR BUSINESS

A sure fire way to get journalists to visit your premises is to have a celebrity come along to a launch or some other event.

Many people either know a celebrity or they have friends or relatives who have connections with them.

It might be a local television newsreader or radio DJ, an actor who has appeared on a television show or an athlete who has achieved something impressive in their sport.

Don't rule out using minor celebrities too. A person who has appeared on a TV reality show or talent contest will play equally well with the media.

If you don't have a friend or relative who has contact details for the celebrity go online to find out the information. It won't be hard to find since they will all more than likely have an agent and a promotional agency.

These are some of the ways you can entice the celebrity to visit your business:

- Launch event for a new product or service
- A relocation launch for your business at the new premises
- The retirement of a long-serving member of staff
- Presentation of a charity cheque for a fundraising event you have organised
- Where a celebrity has recently published a book you can offer them

a public venue for a book-signing event

- When you have scheduled a date and time for the celebrity to appear, give the local press plenty of advance warning.

If you leave it until the day before, a newspaper may well have already committed to other assignments and may be unable to get a freelance photographer to cover your event.

Check with the celebrity if they are happy to be interviewed by reporters and if they would prefer a group press conference or one-to-one interviews.

Take your own camera and make sure you get plenty of good photographs of the celebrity with yourself, your staff and customers.

Not only can you then offer these to the press as additional shots to the ones they have taken themselves they can also be posted on your various social media channels.

Make sure you publicise the celebrity's visit on your website and on social media and include a hashtag with their name and a reference to their Twitter or Instagram name so fans can pick up on the coverage.

This kind of initiative can really help raise the profile of a business, not only on a local level but potentially nationally too, depending on the importance of the celebrity of course.

The final section of this book contains some templates to help you write press releases and blogs.
If you follow the structure for the press releases it will give you a brilliant chance of having them published in newspapers and magazines.
The blog-writing templates will enable you to produce great blogs to engage readers online and influence them to share them across a wide audience.

EXTRA RESOURCES

Templates for writing great press releases & business blogs

www.prforsmallbiz.com

THE STRUCTURE OF A PRESS RELEASE

If you look at press releases from businesses in a wide range of industries and professions they will look pretty similar.

There is a DNA running through them which is common to all. It's a format which journalists recognise and, as such, you should be looking to replicate it in every press release you send out.

At the start of the book I listed the key elements in every press release and they are repeated again below:

- A company logo at the top

- A headline to grab the attention of a journalist

- The date the release is being sent out and details of any embargo, if you want them to use it only after a certain date

- A strong introductory two or three paragraphs explaining what the release is about and why it is newsworthy

- The main body of the release with some good strong quotes (in normal language and not containing jargon or repetitive mentions of your business name)

- Contact details for yourself with an invitation for the journalist to get in touch with you if they require more information

- A caption containing names and subject matter (if a photograph is attached with the press release)

- 'Editor's Notes' containing more detailed information about the subject matter of the release (this element is optional)

- What is known as 'a boilerplate' at the bottom with basic information about your business, such as when it was founded, where it is based, what products and services it sells. Keep this brief though – no more than three sentences

Now let's look at three fictitious businesses from contrasting industries and how they should go about sending out a press release.

SAMPLE PRESS RELEASE TEMPLATES

Sample press release 1

The King's Head – a gastropub based in a rural location in England.
Press release content: To celebrate the 50th anniversary of the pub being built, prices will be charged at the same rates as 50 years ago for a 'happy hour' between 6pm and 7pm.

Logo
The King's Head

Headline
Pub charges 10p a pint to celebrate 50th birthday

Date
August 23rd, 2016

Introductory paragraphs
Customers at The King's Head, in Oxdown, will be charged just 10p a pint to celebrate the 50th anniversary of the pub being built.
Landlord Gordon Barnes is offering food and drink at his gastropub at 1966 prices for a special 'happy hour' on Tuesday (August 30).
But you have to visit the Main Street pub between 6pm and 7pm and in the restaurant it will be first-come-first-served for the 15 tables.

Main body
Mr Barnes, who has run the business with wife Helen for nine years, said: "We wanted to do something special to mark the 50th anniversary.
"So we thought it would be a great idea to bring in 1966 prices for a limited period.
"It's gone down really well with the regulars – some of them have already taken the day off work so they can be here nice and early for the happy hour."
The pub was originally built to serve shoppers at the nearby Pall Mall shopping centre, which dates back to the early 1960s.
It has only had three licensees. The first landlord and landlady, Fred and Beryl Pardew, ran it for 26 years before Tim and Pamela Taylor took over.
Mr and Mrs Barnes have put together displays of photographs showing life

at the pub going back to 1966.

He added: "I've got a feeling we will be packed out for the happy hour but it's a special occasion so I hope people come along and celebrate with us."

Caption

Photo (attached) shows Gordon and Helen Barnes with a blackboard showing the 1966 prices they will be charging to celebrate The King's Head's 50th birthday.

Contact details

For more information about the pub and its 50th birthday celebrations, telephone Mr Barnes on Oxdown 732711 or email him on Gordon@kingshead.co.uk

Boilerplate

The King's Head is a gastropub which was built in Oxdown in 1966. Gordon and Helen Barnes have been landlord and landlady for nine years. The pub has a busy restaurant and an award-winning chef called Stephen Parkinson. The King's Head also has a large beer garden and parking for 36 cars.

Sample press release 2

Blooming Marvellous – a florist shop based on a town centre high street. Press release content: The shop is opening soon and will be the only florists in the small market town of Oxdown.

Logo
Blooming Marvellous

Headline
New florist shop set to open in Oxdown

Date
September 1st, 2016

Introductory paragraphs
Residents at Oxdown will soon have somewhere to buy their flowers in the town again when Blooming Marvellous opens up on Monday (September 5th).
The shop, which is on High Street opposite the doctors' surgery, will stock flowers for weddings and funerals as well as general bouquets and pot plants.
The owner is Samantha Quenby (26), who was born and brought up in the town.

Main body
Miss Quenby said: "I am a fully qualified florist and my dream has always been to open my own shop.
"When the old shoe shop closed down in High Street I just thought it would be the ideal location for me.
"I believe it's a shop that people in Oxdown desperately need. They have not had anywhere to buy flowers in the town since Bell Flowers closed down three years ago."
Miss Quenby, who will be assisted by two full-time members of staff, plans to offer deliveries to customers as well as selling in her shop.
She added: We already have lots of orders and we haven't opened yet. I have been asked to do the flowers for three weddings in September, a funeral and a 75th birthday party."

Contact details

For more information about Blooming Marvellous, telephone Miss Quenby on Oxdown 732651 or email her on sam@bloomingmarvellous.co.uk

Boilerplate

Blooming Marvellous is a florists based in Oxdown. It opened for business in September 2016 and is owned by Samantha Quenby. The shop specialises in providing flowers for family occasions such as weddings, funerals, Christenings and birthday parties. It also offers a delivery service as well as sales of bouquets and pot plants in the shop.

Sample press release 3

The Physio Centre – a physiotherapy practice which specialises in rehabilitation from sports injuries.
Press release content: The business has been asked to give physiotherapy to members of the Team GB Olympic gymnastics squad, which is based nearby.

Logo
The Physio Centre

Headline
Oxdown physios asked to treat Olympic gymnasts

Date
September 11th, 2016 – EMBARGOED until September 15th. 2016

Introductory paragraphs
Physios based at Oxdown are to treat Team GB's Olympic gymnasts to ensure they are in perfect shape for the next international competition.
Beth Sainsbury, Harriet Holding and Dave Garner, who are partners in The Physio Centre on Baldrick Street, were approached by the squad's coaches last month.
They will be required to give sports massage before and after training sessions at nearby Loxton Gymnastics Club, as well as organising rehabilitation programmes when the gymnasts suffer injuries.

Main body
Beth, who started the business with her colleagues six years ago, was delighted to be asked to carry out the work.
She said: "It was a massive surprise, to be honest. We watched the squad compete at the Olympics this summer and we never dreamed we would be asked to treat them. It's very exciting for us and to be asked to do this is great for our reputations as physios."
The Physio Centre, which started up in the premises formerly occupied by Halton's Dental Surgery, is open six days a week, 9am to 5.30pm Monday to Friday and 9am to 12.30pm on Saturdays.
Dave, who was an international swimmer for Great Britain as a teenager, is looking forward to working with the gymnasts.

He said: "It was always my dream to go to the Olympics but I suppose working with the gymnasts will be the next best thing.

"They have a European Championships coming up early next year so we will be working hard to make sure they are all fit and ready for that."

Please note there is an embargo on this press release – it must not be published until September 15th, 2016 at the earliest.

Contact details
For more information about The Physio Centre or to organise a photograph, telephone Oxdown 732444 or email info@thephysiocentre.co.uk

Boilerplate
The Physio Centre is a physiotherapy practice based on Baldrick Street in Oxdown. The three partners involved in the business are Beth Sainsbury, Harriet Holding and Dave Garner. They specialise in sports massage and rehabilitation programmes following injuries and operations. Treatment of sports injuries is also a speciality.

Please note these press releases would not include the headings for each section when they are sent out. They are there merely to show you the various component parts of an archetypal press release.

HOW TO WRITE GREAT BUSINESS BLOGS

Many, many business people start off writing a blog to showcase what they do. But a lot of them lose interest after two or three posts because hardly anyone is reading them.

So why is that?

Often it is because their blogs are not visible enough online. There are apparently two million blog posts published every day so intense competition is one reason why yours might not be getting the traction you hoped for.

So the aim for you when you publish a blog is to make sure people see it in the first place and then stick around to read it after scanning the headline.

The good news is that there are certain things you can do to make your blog visible to people online and, more importantly, existing and potential customers.

Address each of the following and you will massively improve the reach of your blog posts every time you publish:

1 Strong Headline
Research has shown that only 20 per cent of people who have clicked on a link to a blog go on to read it after they've seen the headline. Clearly, the words you use in your heading are crucial to ensuring your post gets read. My advice would be to make it as clear and concise as you can so readers know what the post is about.
But also add an element which indicates you are solving a problem or telling your audience something unusual or unique. Numbers also work well, such as '10 top tips to …' or '5 ways to improve your…'.

2 A Unique Angle
The subject matter is key to drawing in your audience. You need to be telling readers something they don't already know. This might be through your own individual insight, a ground-breaking product or service you provide or just a strong opinion on a topical issue.

3 Solve a Problem
Your blog should aim to provide an answer to a challenge or a problem. Think about helping people with your post. A cleaner could give away tips on getting rid of a particularly deep stain, a chef could give advice on how to make a certain dish and a fitness instructor might list exercises to help people strengthen stomach muscles.

4 Make it Readable
Think about your own experiences of clicking on a link to a blog which sounds interesting just by reading the headline. Then you see the post and it looks about 1,000 words long. It's a turn-off isn't it?
Most blogs should be between 250 and 400 words long because we all have notoriously short attention spans online. Other tips to entice people to read your blog are to write in short paragraphs, bold up certain words, convert some words to italics and, to break up the text, add sub-headings and bullet points where you can.

5 Include an Image
A good photograph or graphic will help draw the reader's eye. If it is strong enough, this image may even entice someone to read your blog on the back of it. Pictures with people in them often prove effective in garnering online interest. People like to read about people, as all young journalists are told. And this is also the case when it comes to blogs. I mentioned earlier in this book about the value in taking a series of generic photographs which can be used to showcase your business. If your blog is about a professional skill you and your employees can demonstrate then show it off with images of them doing it.

6 Avoid the Hard Sell
People are not going to read a blog if it comes across like an advert, singing the praises of your company and its products and services. Your aim is to make your post informational and interesting. You can still promote what you do by stealth. Write about issues and topics relevant to your business to help establish you as a voice of authority in your industry. And highlight problems which your business can solve for customers without going overboard about how brilliant you are. You can add a link to your website at the end so people associate the content with your products and services.

7 Optimise your SEO
This is essential in making your blogs visible to a wider audience. SEO is the abbreviation for Search Engine Optimisation and basically refers to actions which make online content easier to find through search engines such as Google.
This means using the Google Keyword Planner tool I talked about earlier in the book to find relevant words and phrases people are searching for.
You should include these in your heading, in the introductory paragraph and in anchor text (phrases which are highlighted and which link through to a website). When you are uploading a photo to your blog also make sure these keywords are in the file name of the image and in the 'alternate text field' when prompted. Try to get people to comment on your blogs too because the greater the interaction the higher they are likely to be in the Google search rankings.

8 Post Links on Social Media
When you are updating your Twitter and Facebook accounts make sure you include a post with a link to your blog. When a post has been freshly written you might want to refer to it on social media at least twice a day. Vary the wording of your content each time so it doesn't get repetitive.
Some small businesses use blogging sites such as WordPress and Blogger as their company website so, in this case, you can include a link to your blog in your profile. Use a scheduling tool such as Hootsuite to post links to blogs at optimum times.
This last point leads us nicely on to the final piece of advice.

9 Schedule Blogs at Optimum Times
Most blogging platforms give you the option to either post immediately or at some time in the future. Clearly, you want your blogs to go live when the majority of your customers and prospective customers are likely to be online.
If you are unsure when this is likely to be then lunchtime (12.30-2pm) is often worth considering since many people surf the net on their mobiles or on work computers during their lunch break.
If you are trying to reach executives or senior managers then 7.30am-8.30am and 6pm-7pm work well because many will be commuting to and from work during those periods. Alternatively, 8pm-10pm is an effective time to post a blog when people are relaxing after dinner and looking at their phones while relaxing.

Structure of a business blog

It can sometimes be daunting when you've set yourself the task of writing a blog but you just can't get started. You've heard of writer's block, well this is a case of blogger's block!

The best way of getting around this problem is to structure your blogs. This will help you focus and ensure you create great content which is going to be widely read.

This should be the basic structure of every blog you write:

- **Heading** - As we've touched on above, the headline should be strong enough to entice people to read your blog

- **Introductory paragraphs** - They find the heading fascinating and they start to read. Now, use dynamic phrases or ask a question in the first few lines to draw readers in further.

- **Main content** - The style should be chatty, with lots of short paragraphs and broken up with sub-headings, bullet points and highlighted passages (most blogging platforms allow you to pull out a quote so it stands out on the page).

- **Concluding paragraphs** - Round your blog off by returning to the subject matter in the headline. Answer a question you posed or reiterate the important parts of the post. This isn't necessary if you are listing top tips or best practice ideas.

- **Call to action** – End by directing readers to your business website by offering them more details about a particular service or product or include an email address for them to contact you if they want further information about something. You should also invite them to comment on your blog.

Sample templates for business blogs

Example 1 – Blog by landlord of village pub, The King's Arms

5 things we love about beer gardens

Imagine you are relaxing on a lovely British summer's day (difficult to imagine most of the year, I know, but stay with me) and you fancy a pint in a country pub (http://www.kingsarmsbeergarden.co.uk/).
The chances are you will want to sit outside and enjoy the sunshine so you will be thinking about the beer gardens in the area.
You will discount those pubs which don't have an outdoor area. Those that have dead flowers and rusty seats will also be discarded.
Most drinkers will consider five key elements when it comes to deciding which beer garden to visit. And here they are:

Nice furniture
This sounds obvious but there are pubs who attempt to cut costs by setting out cheap or ageing tables and chairs.
Beer gardens should have good comfortable seats which are cleaned regularly. Customers want to relax and enjoy the sunshine with the option to put up a sunshade if it gets too hot. And it is important that staff don't leave dirty glasses and plates for new customers who arrive. Tables should be cleared regularly.

Pitchers
When you are sitting outside enjoying a pint or two, you don't want the hassle of having to go back inside to visit the bar. Especially if there is a group of you. A great way around this problem is when customers are offered pitchers of beer. These can hold four or five pints which mean customers can spend a lot more time enjoying the sunshine.
It doesn't have to be just beer either. Jugs of Pimms or cider work just as well.

Attractive garden
Pub landlords who care about their beer garden plan ahead. They start thinking about the grass and the plants well ahead of the summer.

By nurturing the garden in the spring, the benefits will be in evidence by the time the thermometer starts rising in June. A few scattered hanging baskets look great too.

Picnic baskets
Drinking outside makes you hungry. Yes, you might opt for a packet of crisps from the bar, a round of sandwiches or a meal from the set menu. But what if you have the option of buying a picnic?
This could be a collection of snacks, sandwiches and other food which you could enjoy in the beer garden, picnic-style.
Pubs which offer picnics on the menu give customers a really nice option, particularly when they are out with the family or with a group of friends.

Smoking areas
Non-smokers won't be happy if they have to share the beer garden with people puffing away all around them. This is particularly the case when customers are enjoying a meal. So it's a good idea when pubs reserve a portion of the outdoor area for people who want a cigarette or a cigar, preferably with some kind of shelter for when the weather turns.

We would love to hear what you enjoy most in your favourite beer garden so please leave a comment below

For more details about the beer garden at The King's Arms go online at www.kingsarmsbeergarden.co.uk

Key points about this blog
Let's take a look at why this blog might be attractive to readers and potential customers.
It's written by the fictitious landlord of a village pub and is aimed at highlighting the quality of the establishment's beer garden.
Those who like a drink love visiting beer gardens in the warmer weather so this is a good way of influencing them to visit this pub.
The blog also helps build the pub's brand and associates it with attractive beer gardens.

The **headline** contains the **keywords** *beer garden* and the use of a number will also attract readers.

The **introductory paragraphs** paint an alluring picture of enjoying a drink on a summer's day.

There is a chatty **style** to the blog which readers will find engaging. **Short paragraphs** and **sub-headings** make it easy to read.

The **promotional** aspect is that each of the five elements can be found at the pub which has initiated the blog.

The phrases '*a pint in a country pub*' and '*Pubs which offer picnics on the menu*', which were identified on the Google Keyword Planner tool as having a high number of online searches, have **hyperlinks** which link through to the pub's website.

Two or three **nice images** of the pub's beer garden should be uploaded into the post with appropriate captions.

The post ends with a **call to action** for readers to leave a comment and the option to find out more about the beer garden at The King's Arms by clicking the link to the pub's website.

Example 2 – Blog by a high street estate agency

6 top tips to help sell your house

So, you need to sell your house and you've enlisted an estate agent to handle the sale.
But you might be asking yourself how can I help sell my property?
Well, quite a lot actually. How you present your home is crucial when it comes to interesting buyers.
First impressions can swing the deal or kill it completely.
Here are our top tips on how to help sell your home:

Repaint your front door
The front door is the first thing a potential buyer will see. Chipped paint or a dull colour may well put them off from the very beginning. So paint the door in an appropriate and vibrant colour a few days before viewings.

Put fresh flowers in the lounge and the kitchen
These will make your house smell nice. And they will also make it feel like a home and somewhere it is comfortable to live. Arrange your flowers in nice vases in the lounge and the kitchen, where most people spend a high proportion of their daytime hours.

Remove clutter
There are hard and fast rules when it comes to how to sell your house. A surefire way of putting off buyers is to leave bin bags and boxes piled up around your home. The same can be said of washing left drying in rooms or folded on chairs. Create a great first impression by getting rid of all clutter. It will also make the inside of the property look bigger.

Do the washing up and leave the work surfaces clear
It is never nice to walk into a stranger's house and see dirty pots and plates piled up in the sink. It makes the kitchen look messy and also gives off a vibe that you are not that bothered about selling your house.

Cut the lawn and tidy up the flower beds
Run the mower over the lawn a day before a viewing and spend some time

getting rid of weeds. If you grow vegetables in the back garden, leave them growing in the soil so you can point them out to potential buyers as another feature of the house.

Make sure pets are out of the house
Some people who view your property may well love dogs or cats. But some won't so don't take the risk of leaving pets in the home during a viewing. There is also the prospect of dogs barking or jumping up at viewers which probably won't go down well.

For more tips on how to sell your home or details on how we can help you sell it, go online at www.rennierealestate.com

Key points about this blog
This blog is aimed at helping vendors sell their homes. The main objective is to align the estate agent's brand with best practice in preparing properties for sale. There is no hard sell and proclamations that their business can sell the reader's home for them. But the content infers that the business knows what it is doing and by establishing itself as a voice of authority some readers will trust it enough to go through to their website and, ultimately, enlist their services for a house sale.

The **heading** is search engine-friendly, it contains strong **keywords** and includes a number to further engage the audience.
The **introductory paragraphs** pose a question which everyone asks themselves when they come to putting their home on the market. This engages the reader and entices them to read further.
The post is **readable** because it is split up into small sections under sub-headings and contains short, sharp sentences.
It provides **useful content** which does not overtly promote the estate agent's brand.
But the reader will associate the best practice contained in it with the professional expertise of the business which is posting the blog.
The **keyword search phrases** which feature high in Google rankings – '*how can I sell my property*' and '*how to sell your house*' – are attached to hyperlinks which readers can click on to go through to the estate agent's website.
There should be two or three **nice images** uploaded into this blog showing, for example, fresh flowers in a lounge, a tidy garden and an uncluttered

kitchen. These pictures can be from properties the estate agent has actually sold or is in the process of selling.

Finally, there is a **call to action** with a link to a web address for the estate agent's website. Email and telephone contact details can also be included here.

PRACTICAL TEST:

While it is fresh in your mind, have a go at writing a blog which showcases your business. Include the elements I have outlined here and follow the structure I described. Then go ahead and post the blog using the tips I gave for maximising the SEO for the post and promote it via social media.

What's next for you?

If you've read every chapter in this book and you've worked through my practical exercises for writing press releases and blogs you will be feeling a lot more confident about promoting your business.

The aim of this book is to help small businesses and start-ups who haven't got a huge budget to work with.

The 66 ideas I have outlined shouldn't cost you anything to implement, other than an investment of your time and effort.

I've always enjoyed helping to raise the profile of fledgling businesses and those with small budgets and I'm hoping that some of that passion has come through in these pages.

I'm really keen to help small businesses make themselves more visible to customers and clients so if you have any questions which aren't answered in this book then feel free to email me at nrennie157@gmail.com and I will pass on my knowledge and advice.

I also run a number of bespoke PR training courses for small businesses, which expand on the principles I've covered here.

These are small training groups in various UK locations where I will go into more depth on some of the content featured in the book.

There will be practical exercises on writing press releases and blogs and I will show you how you can set your business up on the various social media channels and operate them effectively to reach more customers.

You will also have the opportunity to ask me for advice on the PR for your own business and receive a bespoke campaign plan, with ideas for press releases and advice on which social media platforms to use and what kind of content works best for you.

For more information on my PR courses for small businesses, feel free to visit my website at:

www.prforsmallbiz.com

If you are on Twitter you can also Tweet me on my personal page **@renster157** or my new dedicated page for small business PR, which is **@smallbizPR_**

I would also be delighted to connect with you on LinkedIn at **uk.linkedin.com/in/NickRennie1** where I often post PR advice for small businesses and links to relevant blogs.

I am also available for one-to-one coaching if you feel you require a more personal development programme. In this instance I can mentor you by working closely with you on your PR.

We can also work on your skills for writing press releases to ensure journalists want to use them and hone your blog-writing technique.
For more details on this package, please email me at nrennie157@gmail.com.

Finally, I would like to wish all of my readers the best of luck in your efforts to promote your businesses using the PR ideas I have given in this book.

Best wishes,
Nick Rennie

Email: nrennie157@gmail.com
Website: www.prforsmallbiz.com
Twitter: @renster157 & @smallbizPR_

Printed in Great Britain
by Amazon